The Future of the Iraqi Popular Mobilization Forces

Lessons from Historical Disarmament, Demobilization, and Reintegration Efforts

DANIEL EGEL, TREVOR JOHNSTON, BEN CONNABLE

Prepared for the Office of the Secretary of Defense
Approved for public release; distribution unlimited

 NATIONAL DEFENSE RESEARCH INSTITUTE

T0002909

For more information on this publication, visit **www.rand.org/t/RRA722-1**.

About RAND

The RAND Corporation is a research organization that develops solutions to public policy challenges to help make communities throughout the world safer and more secure, healthier and more prosperous. RAND is nonprofit, nonpartisan, and committed to the public interest. To learn more about RAND, visit www.rand.org.

Research Integrity

Our mission to help improve policy and decisionmaking through research and analysis is enabled through our core values of quality and objectivity and our unwavering commitment to the highest level of integrity and ethical behavior. To help ensure our research and analysis are rigorous, objective, and nonpartisan, we subject our research publications to a robust and exacting quality-assurance process; avoid both the appearance and reality of financial and other conflicts of interest through staff training, project screening, and a policy of mandatory disclosure; and pursue transparency in our research engagements through our commitment to the open publication of our research findings and recommendations, disclosure of the source of funding of published research, and policies to ensure intellectual independence. For more information, visit www.rand.org/about/principles.

RAND's publications do not necessarily reflect the opinions of its research clients and sponsors.

Published by the RAND Corporation, Santa Monica, Calif.
© 2023 RAND Corporation
RAND® is a registered trademark.

Library of Congress Cataloging-in-Publication Data is available for this publication.

ISBN: 978-1-9774-0716-0

Cover: Mahmoud Hosseini/Creative Commons.

About This Report

This report presents an analysis of historic cases of disarmament, demobilization, and reintegration (DDR) to inform present U.S. policy on Iraq's Popular Mobilization Forces (PMF). The PMF represent a threat to both Iraqi sovereignty and U.S. policy interests, given that several of these militias retain ties to Iran and many PMF fighters remain loyal to their former commanders despite being formally integrated into the Iraqi armed forces in 2016. Findings from this analysis are intended to inform current and future American policies on the PMF.

The research reported here was completed in April 2021 and underwent security review with the sponsor and the Defense Office of Prepublication and Security Review before public release.

RAND National Security Research Division

This research was sponsored by the Office of the Secretary of Defense and conducted within the International Security and Defense Policy Program of the RAND National Security Research Division (NSRD), which operates the National Defense Research Institute (NDRI), a federally funded research and development center sponsored by the Office of the Secretary of Defense, the Joint Staff, the Unified Combatant Commands, the Navy, the Marine Corps, the defense agencies, and the defense intelligence enterprise.

Human Subject Protections (HSP) protocols were used in this study in accordance with the appropriate statutes and DoD regulations governing HSP. Additionally, the views of the sources rendered anonymous by HSP are solely their own and do not represent the official policy or position of DoD or the U.S. government.

For more information on the RAND International Security and Defense Policy Center, see www.rand.org/nsrd/isdp or contact the director (contact information is provided on the webpage).

Summary

In this report, we examine lessons learned from previous efforts toward disarmament, demobilization, and reintegration (DDR) of former combatants and militia forces to inform U.S. government policy on the Iraqi Popular Mobilization Forces (PMF). The PMF played a critical role in the fight against the Islamic State. But this paramilitary force now represents a challenge to civil-military relations, given that many PMF fighters remain loyal to their former commanders despite being formally integrated into the Iraqi armed forces in 2016. Further, because many of these militias retain ties to Iran, the PMF's integration into Iraq's security services provides Iran with a new opportunity to undermine U.S. interests and subvert Iraq's struggling democratic government. Addressing the challenges posed by the PMF will be essential to the success of any U.S. strategy in Iraq and the broader Middle East.

We analyze historic DDR programming to assess whether a U.S.-supported DDR effort in Iraq might succeed. We seek to answer two central questions:

1. How often are internationally supported DDR programs successful in reducing the power and influence of groups like the PMF?
2. Under what conditions and to what extent could such DDR programs be effective in Iraq?

Our analysis of previous DDR efforts builds on a historical analysis of internationally supported DDR programs from 1979 to 2010. Through a review of 30 historical DDR programs, we identify five case studies of DDR programs targeting groups similar to the PMF. A detailed analysis of these case studies allows us to derive lessons that can inform current options.

Our historical analysis indicates that DDR focused on the PMF will be extremely difficult unless linked to complementary security sector reform (SSR) and political reforms that provide greater inclusion. Further, DDR programming pushed by the United States is anticipated to be particularly problematic and likely to backfire. Pressure from American leaders against the PMF would give Iranian-backed PMF leaders a rallying cry to regain some of their dwindling prestige and to divert some negative attention away from Iran. Direct U.S. intervention would also shift negative public attention in Iraq from the PMF to the United States, further undermining U.S. influence. While reducing Iranian-backed PMF power and influence might be beneficial to the United States, a policy that seeks to force that reduction might, in fact, have the opposite effect.

Contents

Figures and Tables

Figures

Tables

CHAPTER ONE

Introduction

With the territorial defeat of the Islamic State, Iraq faces a number of thorny political and security challenges to post-conflict stability. Perhaps none is more consequential or contentious than the future of the Popular Mobilization Forces (PMF). The PMF played a critical role in the fight against the Islamic State and rose to public prominence in Iraq as a result. Now, this loose constellation of paramilitary groups, many of which have divided loyalties, represents a challenge to Iraqi civil-military relations.[1]

While most of the PMF groups were formally integrated into the Iraqi armed forces in 2016, many fighters remain loyal to their former militia commanders, some of whom are, as of early 2021, powerful elected officials.[2] This integration has given Iran, which has overt influence over several prominent PMF groups, the ability to manipulate and potentially hobble some of the critical functions of Iraq's democracy, including parliamentary representation and oversight.[3] In addition, PMF groups have attacked U.S. and allied personnel in Iraq and used their political and military power to erode Western influence. Both Iraqi and Western leaders have openly acknowledged that this situation is untenable,[4] but clear and timely solutions are not readily apparent.

This potential threat to peace is a common problem in the wake of civil conflict. Soldiers and leaders from nonstate armed groups often have few viable alternatives to continuing armed struggle.[5] The broad set of activities designed to address this post-conflict challenge is typically referred to as *disarmament, demobilization, and reinte-*

---

[1] Crispin Smith, "Iraq's Raid on Iran-Backed Militias: Is the New Prime Minister Ready to Rein Them In?" *Just Security*, July 16, 2020.

[2] Inna Rudolf, *The Hashd's Popular Gambit: Demystifying PMU Integration in Post-IS Iraq*, London: International Centre for the Study of Radicalisation, King's College London, 2019.

[3] Ben Connable, "Iraq's Vote to Expel U.S. Troops Is Iran's True Victory," *Los Angeles Times*, January 5, 2020b.

[4] These comments were made by senior Iraqi and American government officials to or, in many cases, in front of one of the authors of this report during various interviews, workshops, conferences, and other convenings from 2017 through 2021. Also see Christopher M. Blanchard, *Iraq: Issues in the 116th Congress*, Washington, D.C.: Congressional Research Service, R45633, updated July 17, 2020.

[5] Jonah Schulhofer-Wohl and Nicholas Sambanis, *Disarmament, Demobilization, and Reintegration Programs: An Assessment*, Sandöverken, Sweden: Folke Bernadotte Academy, 2010, p. i.

DDR Programs: Scope and Objectives

DDR programs comprise a broad set of activities designed to address post-conflict threats to peace. These programs typically begin by disarming and demobilizing ex-combatants through a series of temporary security arrangements, such as quartering soldiers and storing and monitoring weapons. Reintegration support complements these demobilization efforts by providing transitional assistance, such as stipends and job opportunities, to former combatants. DDR tends to be narrowly focused on short-term objectives and concrete measures to reduce the recurrence of violence.

gration (DDR) programs. Notwithstanding decades of varying experiences with DDR efforts around the world, the academic and policy debate on DDR remains contentious. There is little consensus on when, where, and why some policies succeed and others fail.[6] These disagreements are reflective of the extraordinary challenges and risks associated with DDR. Even the best-designed DDR program may ultimately fail because of the complexity and unpredictability of conflict and post-conflict environments.

In this report, we analyze historic DDR cases to assess the prospects of such programs in Iraq and whether they could help mitigate the threat posed by the PMF. We ask two core questions:

1. How often are internationally supported DDR programs successful in resolving challenges (e.g., reducing the power and influence) of groups like the PMF?
2. Under what conditions and to what extent could such DDR programs be effective in Iraq?

We begin by briefly describing conditions in Iraq and the position of the PMF as of this writing. We then discuss the limits of U.S. presence and leverage in Iraq. Next, we define DDR and its conceptual scope, placing it in context with other related efforts, such as SSR. We conclude the chapter with a brief summary of the report's organization.

---

[6]   For a broader discussion on DDR and security sector reform (SSR) applications in practice, see Christopher von Dyck, *DDR and SSR in War-to-Peace Transition*, London: Ubiquity Press, 2016.

SSR Programs: Scope and Objectives

While related, and often pursued in parallel to DDR, *SSR programs* represent a distinct set of efforts that typically include structural reforms, organizational changes, professional military education, training, and other forms of security force development that may take years or even decades to complete. These programs usually serve as complements to DDR, focusing on the deeper institutional problems (e.g., human rights, the rule of law, civilian control over the military) that short-term DDR policies are not designed to address.

The Rise of the PMF and Its Position in the Iraqi Security Sector

In 2014, four divisions of the Iraqi Army and much of its Federal Police force collapsed as Islamic State militants rolled across the country.[7] Both Baghdad and Erbil were placed under direct threat of assault. Given the absence of credible state security forces, Shi'a Grand Ayatollah Sistani issued a *fatwa*, or religious proclamation, calling for the mobilization of male Shi'a Iraqi civilians to either join existing militia groups, such as the Badr Corps, or form new units to push back the extremist forces. Tens of thousands of primarily Shi'a Arab volunteers rushed into combat.[8] Together, this disparate group of militias became known as the PMF.

The PMF played a significant and public role in the defense against the Islamic State. Militiamen were instrumental in several major Islamic State defeats early in the campaign. Many Iraqis—most prominently, Shi'a Arab Iraqis from the southeast of the country—view the PMF as heroes. Many also believe that the PMF are a necessary security buffer against both internal and external threats to the nation. Demonstrated weaknesses in the Iraqi Army and Federal Police feed the ongoing support for the PMF.

Iraq's government has de jure control over most elements of the PMF, whose core militias were officially brought into the government under a series of decrees beginning

---

[7] Michael Knights, *The Long Haul: Rebooting U.S. Security Cooperation in Iraq*, Washington, D.C.: Washington Institute for Near East Policy, January 22, 2015.

[8] A Sunni Arab tribal militia force (TMF), which is not the focus of this report, does not pose similar challenges to the central government.

in 2016.[9] However, it is widely recognized that PMF militiamen answer primarily to their own leaders and, in some cases, to Iranian advisors.[10]

During 2020, fissures within the PMF began to emerge after a U.S. strike near the Baghdad airport targeting the Iranian Quds commander Qassem Soleimani also killed the influential PMF commander Abu Mahdi al-Muhandis.[11] The Kata'ib al-Hezbollah element within the PMF, which was led by al-Muhandis and had been Iran's go-to proxy in Iraq, was particularly affected by this strike. Al-Muhandis' death precipitated a leadership struggle within this element and the PMF more broadly.[12] These fissures began to gradually deepen throughout 2020, with PMF-linked elements declaring that they would respond to leadership only from the prime minister.[13]

Iraq does not publish official numbers, but analysts estimate that the PMF consists of between 40,000 and 100,000 fighters.[14] These fighters are spread across multiple groups with varying local, sectarian, and political interests. Some groups exist outside the official PMF structure. The most powerful groups, including the Badr Corps, Asa'ib Ahl al-Haq, and Kata'ib al-Hezbollah, are backed by Iran (see Table 1.1 for a summary of the major groups, their leaders, and the years of their formation).[15] Several thousand fighters belong to Sunni Arab or smaller minority groups.

---

[9]   For more on the laws and decrees governing the PMF, see Michael Knights, *Popular Mobilization Force Reform in Iraq: Reintegration or Consolidation of Militia Power?* Washington, D.C.: Washington Institute for Near East Policy, July 8, 2019a; Philippe Atallah, *The Future of the Iraqi Popular Mobilization Forces*, Philadelphia, Pa.: Foreign Policy Research Institute, August 19, 2019; "Iraqi Parliament Passes Contested Law on Shi'ite Paramilitaries," Reuters, November 26, 2016; "Iraq's Shi'ite Militias Formally Inducted into Security Forces," Reuters, March 8, 2018; and Michael Knights, *Helping Iraq Take Charge of Its Command-and-Control Structure*, Washington, D.C.: Washington Institute for Near East Policy, September 30, 2019c.

[10]   Rudolf, 2019.

[11]   Ranj Alaaldin, *What Will Happen to Iraqi Shiite Militias After One Key Leader's Death?* Washington, D.C.: Brookings Institution, March 3, 2020.

[12]   Crispin Smith, "After Soleimani Killing, Iran and Its Proxies Recalibrate in Iraq," *Just Security*, February 27, 2020; John Davison and Ahmed Rasheed, "Fractures Grow Among Iraq Militias, Spell Political Retreat," Reuters, April 1, 2020.

[13]   "After Soleimani and Muhandis, Pro-Iranian Factions in Iraq Are Weakened, Divided," *Arab Weekly*, June 12, 2020.

[14]   Actual numbers are uncertain and probably cannot be known, given the loose monitoring of these groups and their proclivity to inflate their numbers. Several good primers and analyses on the PMF have been published since 2014—for example, Michael Knights, "Iran's Expanding Militia Army in Iraq: The New Special Groups," *CTC Sentinel*, Vol. 12, No. 7, August 2019b.

[15]   A considerable volume of articles and formal research reports has been published on the PMF in the past five years. Many of these have been cited in the main body of this report. We recommend the analyses from the Washington Institute for Near East Policy, as well as insights provided by Renad Mansour in various published articles from 2018 to 2019. See the following for further resources: Michael Eisenstadt and Michael Knights, "Mini-Hizballahs, Revolutionary Guard Knock-Offs, and the Future of Iran's Militant Proxies in Iraq," *War on the Rocks*, May 9, 2017; Omar Al-Nidawi, *The Growing Economic and Political Role of Iraq's PMF*, Washington, D.C.: Middle East Institute, May 21, 2019; Hamdi Malik, *The Future of Iraq's Popular Mobilization Forces*, Wash-

Table 1.1
Major PMF Groups and Their External Support

Group	Leader	Year of Establishment	Association
Asa'ib Ahl al-Haq	Qais al-Khazali	2006	Iran
Badr Organization	Hadi al-Ameri	1982	Iran
Harakat al-Nujaba	Akram al-Ka'abi	2013	Iran
Nineweh Guard	Atheel al-Nujaifi	2014	Sunni Arab
Kata'ib al-Hezbollah	Abu Mahdi Al-Muhandis	2007	Iran
Saraya al-Salam	Muqtada al-Sadr	2003	Shi'a Arab
Saraya al-Khorasani	Sayyid Ali al-Yasiri	2013	Iran

SOURCE: Data are from Dylan O'Driscoll and Dave van Zoonen, "The Future of Iraq: Is Reintegration Possible?" *Middle East Policy*, Vol. 24, No. 3, Fall 2017.

As of early 2021, there are four major pillars in Iraq's security sector: (1) the PMF, (2) the Counter-Terrorism Service (CTS), (3) the Iraqi Army, and (4) the Federal Police.[16] The CTS is an elite counterterror unit that led the counter–Islamic State fight. It has approximately 20,000 soldiers, and it reports directly to the Iraqi Prime Minister. The Iraqi Army is Iraq's oldest and most venerated force, but it has a mixed record of effectiveness.[17] Its approximately 150,000 soldiers are generally seen as being

---

ington, D.C.: Carnegie Endowment for International Peace, September 21, 2017; Ranj Alaaldin, *Containing Shiite Militias: The Battle for Stability in Iraq*, Doha, Qatar: Brookings Doha Center, 2017; Mohammad Al-Iraqi, "Iran and Armed Militias in Post-ISIS Iraq," *Journal for Iranian Studies*, Vol. 1, No. 3, June 2017; John Hannah, "Iran-Backed Militias Are in Iraq to Stay," *Foreign Policy*, July 31, 2019; Renad Mansour, "More Than Militias: Iraq's Popular Mobilization Forces Are Here to Stay," *War on the Rocks*, April 3, 2018; Renad Mansour, "Reining in Iraq's Paramilitaries Will Just Make Them Stronger," *Foreign Policy*, July 9, 2019; and Erica Gaston and András Derzsi-Horváth, *Iraq After ISIL: Sub-State Actors, Local Forces, and the Micro-Politics of Control*, Berlin, Germany: Global Public Policy Institute, March 2018.

[16] Other organizations include the Emergency Response Divisions, local police, and various quick-reaction forces assigned directly to Iraqi ministries.

[17] There is a broad literature on the effectiveness of the Iraqi Army. For examples, see Pierre Razoux, *The Iran-Iraq War*, trans. Nicholas Elliott, Cambridge, Mass.: Belknap Press of Harvard University Press, 2015; Williamson Murray and Kevin M. Woods, *The Iran-Iraq War: A Military and Strategic History*, Cambridge, UK: Cambridge University Press, 2014; Pesach Malovayny, *Wars of Modern Babylon: A History of the Iraqi Army from 1921 to 2003*, Lexington, Ky.: University Press of Kentucky, 2017; Dilip Hiro, *The Longest War: The Iran-Iraq Military Conflict*, London: Grafton Books, 1989; Rob Johnson, *The Iran-Iraq War*, London: Palgrave-Macmillan, 2011; Anthony Cordesman and Abraham R. Wagner, *Lessons of Modern Warfare*, Vol. IV: *The Gulf War*, Boulder, Colo.: Westview Press, 1996; James W. Pardew, Jr., "The Iraqi Army's Defeat in Kuwait," *Parameters*, Vol. 21, No. 4, Winter 1991–1992; Stephen Biddle, "Victory Misunderstood: What the Gulf War Tells Us About the Future of Conflict," *International Security*, Vol. 21, No. 2, Fall 1996; Faleh A. Jabar, "Chapter 6: The Iraqi Army and Anti-Army: Some Reflections on the Role of the Military," *Adelphi Papers*, Vol. 43, No. 354, 2003; Alfred B. Prados, *Iraqi Challenges and U.S. Military Responses: March 1991 Through October 2002*, Washington, D.C.: Congres-

far less effective than those in the CTS and PMF,[18] and the Army is worse-equipped than either of these other forces. Iraq's Federal Police are a paramilitary organization of approximately 25,000 personnel. Requirements for more combat forces after its 2014 collapse necessitated that the Federal Police focus on paramilitary operations at the expense of their traditional policing roles.

Figure 1.1 depicts the relative power, control, resources, and influence of these four security forces as of late 2020. It shows the CTS and PMF in competition at the top, with the Army and Federal Police lagging. This post–Islamic State security environment is indicative of a state that is struggling to gain and maintain control of its security services. Neither the CTS nor PMF falls under the de facto control of an Iraqi ministry, like the Ministry of Defense or the Ministry of Interior. Therefore, these groups operate with limited oversight and are effectively exempt from the standard competition for state resources that affect the Army and police.

Figure 1.1
Competitive Security Environment in Iraq in Early 2021

IMAGE SOURCES: Top left, U.S. Army photo by Sgt. William Parsons; top right, Dishad Anwar, Voice of America; center, U.S. Army photo by Staff Sgt. Adriana Diaz-Brown; bottom, DoD photo by Army Spc. Torrance Saunders.

---

sional Research Service, RL31641, November 20, 2002; and Stephen T. Hosmer, *Why the Iraqi Resistance to the Coalition Invasion Was So Weak*, Santa Monica, Calif.: RAND Corporation, MG-544-AF, 2007.

[18]   There are few known, accurate, unclassified sources on Iraqi order of battle, and none that were up to date as of late 2019. For relevant information, see Jessa Rose Dury-Agri, Omer Kassim, and Patrick Martin, *Iraqi Security Forces and Popular Mobilization Forces: Orders of Battle*, Washington, D.C.: Institute for the Study of War, December 2017.

U.S. Policy and Presence in Iraq

U.S. policy toward Iraq has two broad purposes. Immediate tactical concerns focus on suppressing residual elements of the Islamic State. These goals generally run parallel to longer-term objectives on promoting Iraqi stability, democracy, and sovereignty. U.S. policy tends to assume that a strong, democratic, and stable Iraq is good for U.S. interests in the region.[19] The PMF's ascendance, however, jeopardizes some of these interests and has forced policymakers to reconsider their policy assumptions and approach to Iraq.

As of early 2021, there are several thousand U.S. military and diplomatic personnel in Iraq. Despite this continued U.S. presence, American diplomats have, by most accounts, far less influence over Iraqi policymakers and official policies in 2020 than they had enjoyed in the past, especially compared with the 2003–2011 time frame. In contrast, Iran appears to enjoy greater influence over Iraqi policymaking these days, especially through its PMF proxies. After the 2018 parliamentary elections, representatives associated with major PMF groups entered the Iraqi government en masse. Of the 329 available seats, the Badr Corps won 22, and Asa'ib Ahl al-Haq won 13. Both of these groups have long-established ties to Tehran. Senior militia leaders also play key roles in Iraqi ministries.[20]

U.S. policy in Iraq now stands at a crossroads, and central to this choice is what to do about the PMF. With U.S. influence diminished and Iraqi political elites divided, there are few options available. Given these constraints, and despite the challenges that Iraq faced in successfully demobilizing the Sons of Iraq,[21] policy debates have focused on the potential for DDR and whether such a program could be feasible in Iraq today.

Several previous studies offer a range of perspectives on the viability of DDR programs targeting the PMF. While one study concludes that "any [DDR] program is unlikely in Iraq at present," another concludes that some type of near-term DDR effort is essential and that these efforts should be community-specific and include both economic opportunities and psychosocial programs for fighters.[22] Others emphasize the

---

[19]   For a detailed accounting of U.S. policy in Iraq from the 1980s through 2021, see Ben Connable, *An Enduring American Commitment in Iraq: Shaping a Long-Term Strategy with Iraqi Army Partners*, Santa Monica, Calif.: RAND Corporation, PE-353-OSD, 2020a.

[20]   For information on parliamentary representation, see Phillip Smyth, *Iranian Militias in Iraq's Parliament: Political Outcomes and U.S. Response*, Washington, D.C.: Washington Institute for Near East Policy, June 11, 2018; Adel Al-Gabouri, *The Role of the Popular Mobilization Forces in the Iraqi Political Process*, Washington, D.C.: Washington Institute for Near East Policy, October 1, 2019; and Ahmed Aboulenein, "Iraqi Rival Groups Both Announce Parliamentary Blocs to Form New Government," Reuters, September 2, 2018.

[21]   Scott Peterson, "Maliki or ISIS? Neither Looks Good to Sunni Awakening Veterans," *CSMonitor*, June 18, 2014; Omar Al-Nidawi and Michael Knights, *Militias in Iraq's Security Forces: Historical Context and U.S. Options*, Washington, D.C.: The Washington Institute for Near East Policy, February 22, 2018.

[22]   Jacqueline Parry and Emily Burlinghaus, *Reintegration of Combatants in Iraq After ISIL*, Institute of Regional and International Studies, American University of Iraq, Sulaimani, April 2019, pp. 1–2 and 8–10.

importance of blending DDR and SSR and that an Iraqi-led DDR program would be "highly productive" if conducted alongside SSR, creating individual opportunities for PMF fighters while encouraging broader governance and political reform.[23] Others are less sanguine about the usefulness of SSR.[24]

This report adds to this discourse by describing historical analogues to the PMF and summarizing whether internationally supported DDR programs targeted at groups like the PMF have been successful and the factors that have mitigated that success (or lack thereof).

Organization of This Report

In Chapter Two, we describe DDR in more detail and then review 30 historical cases of DDR. For each case, we identify which groups were the focus of DDR programs and describe the degree to which they resemble the PMF in terms of several key characteristics. We also code the relative success of DDR programs, evaluating the impact on the targeted groups and noting whether violence resumed. The appendix complements this chapter, providing additional insights into these cases and our research methodology.

Having coded these cases, in Chapter Three we then select five groups that closely resemble the PMF and its position in Iraq today from the coded cases. We conduct short case studies on these five groups, exploring key elements of DDR policy and how political and security conditions challenged program implementation and their coordination (if any) with related SSR efforts. Through these case studies, we discuss a range of different possible pathways for the PMF. Finally, in Chapter Four, we provide findings derived from our research.

---

[23] Quote is from Vanda Felbab-Brown, "Pitfalls of the Paramilitary Paradigm: The Iraqi State, Geopolitics, and Al-Hashd Al-Shaabi," policy brief, Washington, D.C.: Brookings Institution, June 2019. O'Driscoll and van Zoonen (2017) similarly conclude that any efforts must include a blend of DDR and SSR and point to failed efforts to integrate the Sunni Awakening fighters into the Iraqi security forces (via DDR programs) as a key factor in the rise of the Islamic State's potency.

[24] Parry and Burlinghaus, 2019.

CHAPTER TWO

DDR Lessons from 30 Historical Cases

This chapter focuses on the first of the two questions posed in this report: *How often are internationally supported DDR programs successful in resolving challenges (e.g., reducing the power and influence) of groups like the PMF?* To do this, we review 30 previous DDR efforts to determine how often these types of programs are successful in mitigating the variety of risks posed by the PMF. These 30 cases represent approximately one-half of all internationally supported DDR programs from 1979 to 2010.[1]

This chapter is divided into two analytical components. The first is focused on identifying which historical DDR efforts targeted groups similar to the PMF and in contexts resembling present-day Iraq. To do this, drawing on a workshop with experts and a review of the literature focused on PMF, we identified five defining characteristics of the PMF problem set, which we use as *selection criteria* in determining the comparability of other groups to the PMF.

The second analytical component is focused on determining the extent to which previous DDR efforts were successful. For each of the 30 cases, we assessed success in two ways. The first was through a qualitative determination, based on a detailed review of the historical literature, of the extent to which the nonstate armed group was successfully reintegrated. The second was whether the group was again involved in violence despite DDR efforts.

Three descriptive findings emerge in this chapter. The first is that the PMF problem set is unusual but not unique; nearly one-half of all DDR cases share four characteristics with the PMF, and three share all five. Second, most DDR cases result in a successful reintegration of a militant group's fighters and a reduced likelihood that the group returns to violence within five years. Third, the historical success of DDR cases,

---

[1] Our analysis includes 23 of the 49 conflicts with internationally supported DDR programs reviewed in Schulhofer-Wohl and Sambanis, 2010. Across these 23 conflicts, a total of 30 different groups were targeted by international DDR efforts, which are the *cases* referred to in this text. As an example, the nearly two-decade-long conflict in Cambodia included DDR efforts involving two major nonstate armed groups (Khmer Rouge and National United Front for an Independent, Neutral, Peaceful and Cooperative Cambodia [FUNCINPEC]). The 23 conflicts included in this analysis were not selected in any deliberate way; instead, we continued to add new conflicts (and groups) until we had achieved sufficient saturation to answer the key research question of this chapter.

especially in terms of fighter reintegration, is somewhat lower among those groups most similar to the PMF (i.e., sharing at least four characteristics in common).

We begin this chapter with an overview of DDR and a comparison of DDR with SSR before turning to this chapter's analytical components. In the next chapter, we focus on the five DDR experiences we judge to be most similar to the PMF and provide a more detailed discussion of why each of those specific DDR efforts succeeded or failed. This qualitative approach to understanding program success provides an in-depth, contextual understanding of the types of challenges most likely to afflict a DDR program targeting the PMF.[2]

Defining Disarmament, Demobilization, and Reintegration

Before discussing the coding criteria and our analysis of historical cases, we begin with a brief discussion of key concepts and definitions. The term *DDR* usually refers to a broad set of activities designed to address post-conflict threats to peace. *Disarmament* is the process of separating weapons from the former combatants who belonged to selected armed groups. *Demobilization* refers to the process of breaking down these armed groups and dismantling their military or paramilitary structures. *Reintegration* focuses on transitioning former fighters from their military roles to civilian roles and, ideally, reducing their propensity to use violence as a means to resolve social, economic, or political grievances. Together, these programs tend to include a series of temporary security arrangements, such as quartering soldiers or storing and monitoring weapons, coupled with such economic incentives as stipends and job opportunities. Mutually reinforcing incentives are designed to encourage ex-combatants to relinquish their arms and return home.

Academic studies of DDR suggest that these programs are most successful when there is a formal, negotiated peace settlement; mutual trust; willingness to engage in the program; and basic security guarantees.[3] While a large number of cases come from war-torn states in Africa, programs have also been implemented in relatively developed countries in Europe, secessionist enclaves in Asia, war-torn parts of South America, and parts of the Middle East.[4] These programs can vary widely in scope, from pro-

---

[2]   To fully parse out the drivers of program success and failure across 30 cases is not only beyond the scope of this study, but it is also unnecessary. Many of these cases represent radically different challenges and contexts from the PMF problem in Iraq. Their lessons, while important and potentially useful, are less valuable to our specific question.

[3]   United Nations Department of Peacekeeping Operations, *Second Generation Disarmament, Demobilization, and Reintegration (DDR) Practices in Peace Operations: A Contribution to the New Horizon Discussion on Challenges and Opportunities for UN Peacekeeping*, New York: United Nations, 2010.

[4]   This paragraph is based largely on the list provided in Table A.1 in Schulhofer-Wohl and Sambanis, 2010.

grams focused on reintegrating child soldiers (e.g., in Sierra Leone) to demobilizing hardened insurgents (e.g., the Taliban in Afghanistan).

Many of these studies and analyses also consider related policies that tend to fall under the umbrella of SSR. While related and often pursued in parallel, DDR and SSR are distinct programs that typically vary in scope, time horizon, and overall approach.[5] As defined previously, DDR tends to be narrowly focused on short-term objectives and concrete measures to reduce the recurrence of violence by disarming and demobilizing ex-combatants. While these efforts may take years to achieve, especially the reintegration phase, DDR is not intended to be a multigenerational program of institutional reform. The focus is on preventing immediate conflict recurrence rather than addressing the underlying political and security conditions that may engender future conflicts.

By contrast, SSR often includes an expansive set of structural reforms, organizational changes, training, and other forms of security force development, which may take years or even decades to complete. In practice, these efforts are often seen as a complement to DDR, focusing on the deeper institutional problems that short-term DDR policies cannot address. SSR programs have ambitious goals, from (re)establishing civilian control over the security sector to protecting human rights and creating structures that defend the rule of law.[6] Among academics and practitioners, debate rages over to what extent and how DRR and SSR efforts should be combined, sequenced, or coordinated.[7]

Analysis of 30 Historical DDR Cases to Inform Iraq Policy

Our analytical approach differs from most previous analyses in that we focus on the groups targeted by DDR rather than on the specifics of the programs. This difference is a consequence of our project's objective: Our intent is to identify nonstate armed groups similar to the PMF and study their trajectory in the wake of DDR efforts.

Our analysis includes 30 different cases, as listed in Table 2.1.[8] We apply a structured coding for each of these groups to identify which are most similar to the PMF, focusing on five key characteristics. And, rather than focusing on broader residual violence across society (as these other researchers have done), we code the impact of DDR on each specific group and whether that group was *involved in* subsequent violence.

---

[5]   Von Dyck, 2016.

[6]   Ursula C. Schroeder and Fairlie Chappuis, "New Perspectives on Security Sector Reform: The Role of Local Agency and Domestic Politics," *International Peacekeeping*, Vol. 21, No. 2, 2014.

[7]   Sean McFate, "The Link Between DDR and SSR in Conflict-Affected Countries," Washington, D.C.: United States Institute of Peace, 2010.

[8]   These 30 cases represent 23 of the 49 conflicts with internationally supported DDR programs reviewed in Schulhofer-Wohl and Sambanis, 2010. In practice, as detailed in Table 2.1 and explained in greater detail in the appendix, DDR efforts often target more than a single group.

Identifying Groups Similar to the PMF: Five Key Characteristics

As we are interested in understanding the likely outcome of DDR on the PMF, our analysis begins by identifying a set of defining characteristics of the PMF. Drawing on a one-day workshop with experts on Iraqi militia forces held at the RAND Corporation's offices in mid-2019 and on the cited literature on the PMF, we identified five characteristics of the PMF problem sets that experts believed to be most germane for understanding the challenges faced in DDR. These characteristics should not be interpreted as independent variables for our analysis of the effectiveness of DDR but rather as a set of selection criteria that we use for identifying other groups most similar to the PMF:

1. Important to National Security

The group is widely perceived by the population to be important for providing security against either an internal or external threat to the nation. The PMF are broadly perceived by Iraqis as a necessary line of defense against a potentially resurgent Islamic State. Neither the Iraqi Army nor the other Iraqi security services are seen as sufficiently capable to defend the state on their own were the PMF to be demobilized and its fighters disarmed.

2. Locally Entrenched

The group enjoys strong support among a geographically concentrated, ethno-sectarian, or other identity-based community that provides substantial political and material support. The PMF are well-established in major cities (e.g., Baghdad, Mosul, Kirkuk) and hold small bases throughout the country. They are the de facto local security force in many parts of Iraq. The PMF enjoy some popularity, and they have legally established themselves in some areas by leasing land and taking other measures to entrench their presence.

3. Roughly Organized but Diverse

The group represents an amalgamation of organizations without a single decisionmaker who can speak for the entire group. The PMF is not a monolith. It comprises a diverse collection of fighters and political-military organizations from primarily Shi'a Arab and some other ethno-sectarian groups. These groups vary in significant ways, including in their core interests, resources and support base, and in their disposition to the United States.

4. Limited Domestic Political Will to Demobilize

Demobilization of the group is not among the most important political priorities for the national government. PMF support extends beyond the street, drawing on a significant number of Iraqi political elites who believe that the PMF, having established a parallel security institution with its own ministry, provide an important counterbalance to U.S. influence in other security forces. Militias are well represented in the Iraqi government. While some Iraqi leaders might wish to demobilize the PMF, they lack sufficient political will or capital to force the issue.

5. Enjoys External Support

The group is supported by an external actor that would be affected by the DDR process and could see its interests threatened. Iranian-backed PMF receive various forms of external support from the Iranian government. Similar international dynamics are present in many other cases.

Building a PMF-Relevant Database of Historical DDR Activities

Table 2.1 summarizes our analysis of the 30 historical DDR cases.[9] The first four columns provide basic background on the conflict, including the country, group, war years, and years of DDR programming. The next five columns summarize our assessment of the similarity of each group to the PMF, based on the five PMF-related characteristics just described. The coding of these five *PMF-Related Characteristics* columns followed a detailed review of each case.[10]

The column titled *Political Trajectory* provides a brief summary of the extent to which the nonstate armed group was formally integrated into either the country's political or its security apparatuses. It describes whether the group was integrated into the armed forces, reconstituted as an accepted political organization, demobilized entirely, or experienced some other outcome.

The last two columns provide a summary of the overall outcomes associated with the DDR efforts. The first of these columns, *DDR Successful?*, provides our overall assessment of whether the nonstate armed group was successfully reintegrated according to the historical material consulted for each group. This column, which provides the overall measure of success that we use in deriving findings from this analysis, draws on the more detailed insights provided in the previous column. In addition, though we do not use this information in the findings in this chapter, the final column (*Recurrence of Violence?*) provides a longer-term measure of success of DDR and SSR efforts by reporting whether the group targeted for DDR was involved in violence within five years of the conclusion of the conflict.[11]

---

[9]   This is based on Schulhofer-Wohl and Sambanis, 2010.

[10]   The appendix provides more details on the sources consulted for each case as well as a summary of the DDR program.

[11]   This column is based on Schulhofer-Wohl and Sambanis, 2010.

Table 2.1
Coded Analysis of 30 Existing DDR Cases

	Country	Group	War Years	DDR Years	PMF-Related Characteristics? 1	2	3	4	5	Political Trajectory	Outcomes Reintegration Successful?	Recurrence of Violence?
1	Afghanistan	Northern Alliance	1996–2001	2003–ongoing	√	√	√	√	√	Leaders individually coopted into political system; fighters incorporated into new or existing security structures	Yes	No
2	—	Taliban	2001–ongoing	2005–ongoing	√	√	√		√	DDR targeting fighters ineffective without peace process	No	Yes
3	Angola	UNITA	1975–1991	1991–1992	√	√	√		√	Group refused to disarm or surrender territory	No	Yes
4	—	UNITA	1992–1994	1995–1998	√	√	√		√	Partial integration into armed forces	Partial	Yes
5	—	UNITA	1997–2002	2002–2008		√	√	√	√	Militant group demobilized and transitioned into a cohesive, competitive political party	Yes	No
6	Bosnia	ARBiH	1992–1995	1996–2006	√	√	√	√	√	Transitioned into new state security system	Partial	No
7	—	HVO	1992–1995	1996–2006	√	√	√	√	√	Transitioned into new state security system	Partial	No
8	—	VRS	1992–1995	1996–2006		√		√	√	Acted as political and military leadership of Serbian enclave before integration into national force	Partial	No
9	Burundi	Tutsi militias	1993–1996	1996–2000		√	√			Integrated into armed services	Yes	Yes

Table 2.1—Continued

	Country	Group	War Years	DDR Years	PMF-Related Characteristics? 1	2	3	4	5	Political Trajectory	Reintegration Successful?	Recurrence of Violence?
10	—	Hutu groups	1993–2006	2000–2006		√		√	√	Joined newly established army or demobilized	Yes	Yes
11	Cambodia	Khmer Rouge[g]	1975–1991	1992–1999					√	Absorbed into armed forces; some later demobilized	Yes	No
12	—	FUNCINPEC[h]	1975–1991	1992		√		√	√	Integrated into new state security system	Yes	No
13	Djibouti	FRUD[i]	1991–1994	1994–1996		√	√		√	Ministerial positions and integrated into army	Yes	No
14	El Salvador	FMLN	1979–1992	1992–1997		√	√	√	√	Demobilized and transitioned into a cohesive, competitive political party	Yes	No
15	Ethiopia	Derg	1974–1991	1991–1997		√				Demobilized	No	No
16	—	EPRDF	1974–1991	1991–1997		√		√	√	Transitioned into a new national army	Yes	No
17	Kosovo	Kosovo Liberation Army	1998–1999	1999–2004	√	√	√	√	√	Leaders individually coopted into political system; fighters incorporated into new or existing security structures	Yes	No
18	Lebanon	Hezbollah	1975–1991	1991	√	√		√	√	Excluded from formal political and security structures, developed parallel institutions that rival the state	No	No
19	Namibia	PLAN	1966–1989	1989–1990	√	√		√	√	20 percent integrated into security services	Partial	No
20	—	SWATF	1974–1989	1989–1990					√	Demobilized	No	No

Table 2.1—Continued

	Country	Group	War Years	DDR Years	PMF-Related Characteristics?					Political Trajectory	Reintegration Successful?	Recurrence of Violence?
					1	2	3	4	5			
21	Nepal	Maoists	1996–2006	2007–2012	√					10 percent integrated into security services, 90 percent paid to retire	Partial	No
22	Nicaragua	Contras	1981–1990	1990–1992		√			√	Demobilized, achieved representation in government	Yes	No
23	Papua New Guinea	BRA and BRF	1988–1997	2001–ongoing		√	√			Independence from Papua New Guinea	Yes	No
24	Tajikistan	UTO	1992–1997	1997–2003	√	√	√	√	√	Integrated into armed forces	Yes	No
25	Uganda	UNLA	1980–1986	1988	√	√			√	Absorbed into armed forces	Yes	Yes
26	—	NRA	1980–1986	1987–1995	√	√			√	Became armed forces of new state	Yes	Yes
27	—	UA, FUNA, UNRF	1980–1985	1986					√	Integrated into armed forces	Yes	No
28	—	WNBF, UNRF II	1994–2002	1997–2002					√	Integrated into armed forces	Yes	No
29	—	LRA	1995–2007	2005–2008					√	Integrated into armed forces (or fled)	Yes	Yes
30	Zimbabwe	RSF, ZANLA, ZIPRA	1964–1979	1980–1985	√	√	√	√	√	Integrated into national army	Yes	Yes

NOTE: UNITA = National Union for the Total Independence of Angola; VRS = Vojska Republike Srpske. See appendix for remaining abbreviations and acronyms.

Findings from Analysis of 30 DDR Cases

The PMF are an unusual group from a historical perspective but certainly not unique. This finding is illustrated in Figure 2.1, which summarizes our coding of the 30 historical cases along the five key PMF characteristics. The left panel in Figure 2.1 reports the total number of cases with characteristics in common with the PMF. Nearly one-half (13 of the 30 cases) have at least four characteristics in common with the PMF. Three groups of 30 share all five characteristics.[12] The rightmost panel summarizes the types of characteristics that are more or less common in historical cases. Unsurprisingly, the PMF's importance to national security is the least common characteristic among other groups, although nearly one-fourth of historical cases share even this characteristic. The two features most commonly shared are local entrenchment and external support.

Historically, most DDR programs result in a successful reintegration of a group's fighters and a reduction in violence, as measured by a group's return to conflict within five years (see Figure 2.2). According to our analysis, more than 60 percent of DDR programs (19 of 30 cases included in this study) resulted in successful reintegration. An additional 20 percent (six of 30 cases) resulted in partial reintegration. In terms of conflict recurrence, 70 percent of groups targeted by DDR programs (21 of 30 cases) were not involved in subsequent violence.

Figure 2.1
Similarity of PMF to Previous Groups Targeted by DDR

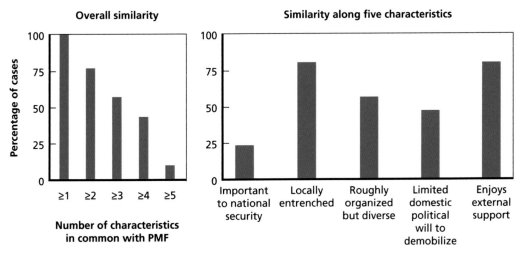

SOURCE: Authors' analysis using data in Table 2.1.

---

[12] Two of these three (KLA and Northern Alliance) are included in the more detailed analysis in the following chapter. We did not include PLAN because it is a much older case.

Figure 2.2
Similarity of PMF to Previous Groups Targeted by DDR

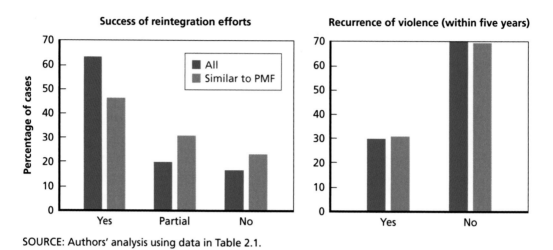

SOURCE: Authors' analysis using data in Table 2.1.

For those groups most like the PMF, specifically the 13 of the 30 cases that share four or five of the PMF-related characteristics, the historical success of DDR programs was somewhat lower. Specifically, though a recurrence of violence among these groups was similarly low (right panel), larger shares of the DDR efforts resulted in either failed or partial reintegration (left panel).

CHAPTER THREE

Lessons from Five DDR Cases

This chapter is focused on addressing the second of the two questions posed in this report: *Under what conditions and to what extent could DDR programs be effective in Iraq?* To answer this question, we provide a series of short case studies to examine how political and security conditions have limited the effectiveness of past DDR efforts targeting groups similar to the PMF. We focus our analysis on the five groups that were identified as the most similar to the PMF as defined by the coding criteria discussed in Chapter Two. While these groups and their contexts resemble the challenge of the PMF in Iraq today, the case studies also provide a broad set of differing experiences with conflict and DDR outcomes.

Collectively, these case studies suggest that, at least in the short term, the demobilization of fighters is extremely difficult unless linked to complementary political and security reforms. There is no fixed formula for success, but our analysis reveals how several factors are especially important, including (1) willingness on the part of the government and the armed group to enter into the process, (2) basic security from violence for both parties, (3) some kind of ready political accommodation available to leadership of the armed group, (4) opportunities for former fighters and leaders that are at least as attractive as the status quo, and (5) the presence of a capable international force ready to assure the security of those being disarmed and demobilized.

In isolation and divorced from complementary SSR efforts, DDR is insufficient. These short-term efforts are unlikely to achieve meaningful change unless domestic and international stakeholders are willing, capable, and patient enough to pursue broader political and structural reform that provides greater inclusion.

Case Selection and Overview

Our case study analysis examined DDR efforts targeted at the following groups: (1) Northern Alliance in Afghanistan, (2) National Union for the Total Independence of Angola (UNITA) in Angola, (3) Farabundo Martí Liberation Front (FMLN) in El Salvador, (4) Kosovo Liberation Army (KLA), and (5) Hezbollah in Lebanon. These five groups, which were drawn from the larger analysis in Chapter Three, comprise a diverse collection of cases falling across five continents and varying in conflict duration. Conflicts also varied by cause, with some beginning after external intervention (Afghanistan), colonial withdrawal (Angola), Marxist insurgency (El Salvador), and ethno-sectarian competition (Lebanon). Although no one group is a perfect comparison with the PMF, these groups collectively capture many of the conditions that make the Iraq case so challenging.

Table 3.1 provides a summary overview of these groups during their conflict years and their similarity to the challenge posed by the PMF. The five columns highlighted as *PMF-Related Characteristics* repeat the coding used in Table 2.1 for identifying historical cases most similar to the PMF. As the table makes clear, these cases closely resemble the PMF, with each group satisfying at least four of the five characteristics. In addition to these characteristics, Table 3.1 also describes the eventual outcome for each post-conflict effort, briefly summarizing the militant group's place within the state's institutional and security structures.

While their post-conflict experiences and trajectories varied in important ways, these cases also share several key features that offer important lessons for Iraq. In the period immediately following conflict, weak and fledgling governments often lack the capacity and political will to push for comprehensive DDR, let alone an expansive SSR agenda. Instead, these governments often pursue a piecemeal DDR approach (e.g., Lebanon) or are forced to offer major concessions to avoid costly confrontation. Rather than disarm the militant group, this conciliatory approach tends to incorporate fighters—often in intact militia units—into new and existing security structures (e.g., Afghanistan).

This more conciliatory approach may, in some cases, incorporate SSR measures, such as institutional reforms that open up the political space for ex-combatants to compete through elections or other formal mechanisms (e.g., Angola and El Salvador). In most cases, this approach helps reduce the risk of conflict recurrence, but it is not devoid of risks for shaky post-conflict governments. If incorporated into the political process, these militant groups rarely threaten the post-conflict order. Instead, they become the main opposition, regularly contesting the incumbent government (e.g., Angola and El Salvador).

By this measure, these groups often come to represent the new order. Having mixed their forces and supporters with existing military and political structures, they have little incentive to destroy the system. But, if excluded, these groups may work outside the state or construct their own parallel governments (e.g., Hezbollah).

In each case study below, we first describe the conflict environment that gave rise to the militant group. We then summarize the major DDR efforts that focused on the group. Finally, we conclude with a brief discussion of the impact, if any, of DDR and other post-conflict political and security reforms on the group.

Table 3.1
Select PMF-Relevant Cases

Country	Group	Conflict Years	National Security (1)	Local Entrenched (2)	Diverse (3)	Limited Political Will (4)	External Support (5)	Long-Term Outcomes
			PMF-Related Characteristics					
Afghanistan	Northern Alliance	2001– ongoing	Yes	Yes	Yes	Yes	Yes	Leaders individually coopted into political system; fighters incorporated into new or existing security structures
Angola	UNITA	1975–2002	No	Yes	Yes	Yes	Yes	Militant group demobilized and transitioned into a cohesive, competitive political party
El Salvador	FMLN	1979–1992	No	Yes	Yes	Yes	Yes	Militant group demobilized and transitioned into a cohesive, competitive political party
Kosovo	KLA	1998–1999	Yes	Yes	Yes	Yes	Yes	Leaders individually coopted into political system; fighters incorporated into new or existing security structures
Lebanon	Hezbollah	1975–1991	Yes	Yes	No	Yes	Yes	Militant group remained excluded from formal political and security structures; the group developed parallel institutions that rival the state

Afghanistan: Northern Alliance

First established in 1992, the Northern Alliance was a coalition of militia forces that played a key role in the defeat of the Taliban in 2001. Drawing fighters from an ethnically and religiously diverse group of forces, the Northern Alliance provided the bulk of the ground combat power in the capture of Kabul, Mazar-e-Sharif, and other key cities.[1] Throughout the 1990s, the Northern Alliance drew on external support from various sources. Western support sharply escalated in late 2001.[2]

Although experts saw a clear need to disarm, demobilize, and reintegrate former combatants, the 2001 Bonn Agreement that built the current Afghan state did not explicitly mention DDR.[3] Northern Alliance commanders initially resisted the demobilization of their forces: Militias represented an extension of their personal power, and commanders were perhaps rightly concerned about retaliation or future shifts in power.[4] Beginning in 2003 and continuing to the present day, a series of DDR and SSR programs has focused on these fighters with varying success.[5]

To encourage demobilization and support these DDR efforts, key leaders in the Northern Alliance were incorporated into the government of President Hamid Karzai. However, Karzai's inclusion of former leaders and groups was selective. He coopted key figures rather than allowing for the formation of a cohesive party or monolithic bloc. In the early years of this process, senior Afghan political leaders made a calculated choice to offer compromises for short-term stabilization.[6] Many fighters were allowed to join the Ministry of Interior while *also* retaining loyalty to their original commanders. Others joined the new Afghan Army. This has had long-term negative consequences for both rule of law and stability.[7] In later years, these commanders slowed the DDR and SSR efforts, leading one analyst to conclude in 2015 that this process had failed to delegitimize militiamen or to eliminate their patronage connections with militia leaders.[8]

Angola: National Union for the Total Independence of Angola

Drawing on support from several geographically dispersed and excluded groups, Jonas Savimbi established UNITA in 1966 in opposition to the Portuguese colonial government.[9] Although Portugal withdrew from Angola in 1975, it only exacerbated ongoing

---

[1]   "Who Are the Northern Alliance?" BBC News, November 13, 2001.

[2]   Douglas M. Johnson, *The Historical Foundations of World Order: The Tower and the Arena*, Leiden, Netherlands: Martinus Nijhoff Publishers, 2008.

[3]   Deedee Derksen, *The Politics of Disarmament and Rearmament in Afghanistan*, Washington, D.C.: United States Institute of Peace, 2015, p. 7.

[4]   Derksen, 2015, pp. 9–11.

[5]   Kate Clark, *Graft and Remilitarisation: A Look Back at Efforts to Disarm, Demobilise, Reconcile, and Reintegrate*, Kabul, Afghanistan: Afghanistan Analysts Network, July 12, 2018.

[6]   Derksen, 2015, p. 12.

[7]   Derksen, 2015, p. 10.

[8]   This analysis was referring to only the diagnostic program, which began in 2005 (Derksen, 2015, p. 12).

[9]   South African History Online, "The Angolan Civil War (1975–2002): A Brief History," webpage, undated.

civil conflict. Savimbi, competing militia leaders, and Savimbi's international allies pivoted to challenge the Cuban- and Soviet-backed government. During the decades of war that followed, UNITA would come to control significant territory in Angola, including regions rich with diamond mines that helped finance its war.[10] Savimbi also received external support from a variety of states, including South Africa and the United States. External financing helped to ensure that Savimbi's movement would sputter along for decades.[11]

Beginning in 1991, the Angolan government pursued a series of failed efforts to end the civil war and begin the DDR process.[12] The first of these efforts sought to integrate opposition forces into a new state military while demobilizing and disarming all other fighters. This effort never made it past the initial quartering of soldiers.[13] UNITA refused to disarm or surrender its territory, and the ceasefire collapsed. The next effort was more ambitious, establishing a new ceasefire and offering senior positions for militia generals. It promised opportunities in the police and Ministry of Interior for its fighters.[14] While the newly formed National Unity Government made significant progress—with some UNITA leaders even holding ministerial positions—the demobilization process lagged. After failing to meet critical deadlines, the DDR process collapsed, and the war reignited in 1998.

Finally, in 2002, following Savimbi's death, UNITA's political and military leadership negotiated an enduring peace agreement. The agreement provided senior government positions for the group's leaders. They declared the movement disarmed and committed to the political process.[15] In exchange for political normalization, this agreement also established new structures to implement and manage the DDR process, beginning with demobilization concentrated around 35 gathering areas for registering and quartering ex-combatants and their families. By early 2007, nearly 100,000 fighters had demobilized.[16] While a small proportion of these fighters were hired by various ministries, most faced difficulties finding work, relying on reintegration assistance from the government and nongovernmental organizations. Some fighters instead turned to private security firms, but this choice has not disrupted the peace.

---

[10] "Unita Rebels Sold Diamonds Worth 4 Billion Dollars," Pan African News Agency, June 27, 2000.

[11] Chris Simpson, "Obituary: Jonas Savimbi, Unita's Local Boy," BBC News, February 25, 2002.

[12] Alex Vines and Bereni Oruitemeka, "Bullets to Ballots: The Reintegration of UNITA in Angola: Analysis," *Conflict, Security and Development*, Vol. 8, No. 2, 2008.

[13] Vines and Oruitemeka, 2008, p. 243.

[14] Vines and Oruitemeka, 2008, p. 245.

[15] Vines and Oruitemeka, 2008, p. 249.

[16] Vines and Oruitemeka, 2008, p. 255.

By 2017, UNITA emerged as Angola's second-largest political party,[17] and it remained so as of early 2021.[18]

El Salvador: Farabundo Martí Liberation Front

In 1980, the FMLN formed out of a collaboration of five different Salvadoran Marxist-Leninist revolutionary organizations.[19] Although there were profound differences among the five organizations, the FMLN unified them under a common platform demanding "the dissolution of the army and security forces; agrarian reform; the dissolution of state powers and the passing of a new constitution."[20] In 1981, with materiel and political support provided by Cuba and the Soviet Union, the FMLN launched a failed offensive against a U.S.-backed government.[21] Despite waning external support, the FMLN would fight an inconclusive, decade-long insurgency.[22]

In January 1992, after nearly two years of negotiations, the FMLN and Salvadoran government signed a peace agreement ending the insurgency. Unlike in other cases, where DDR proceeded in fits and starts until these efforts were complemented by other structural reforms, the FMLN agreed to demobilize and transform into a political party by the end of 1992. But it had sufficient residual power to make this process conditional on the government implementing a series of reforms specified in the peace accord.[23] These reforms were expansive in scope, including changes to the

---

[17] Stephen Eisenhammer, "Angola's Ruling Party Declared Election Winner as Opposition Cries Foul," Reuters, August 25, 2017.

[18] Graciosa Silva, "General Elections: Opposition Committed to a Coalition That Changes the Course of Democracy 45 Years Later," *Ver Angola*, January 14, 2021.

[19] These subordinate organizations had formed during the 1970s and 1980s to resist the political repression of El Salvador's authoritarian regime.

[20] Alberto Martín Álvarez, *From Revolutionary War to Democratic Revolution: The Farabundo Martí National Liberation Front (FMLN) in El Salvador*, Berlin, Germany: Berghof Conflict Research, Transitions Series No. 9, November 1, 2010, p. 17.

[21] "Excerpts From Haig's Briefing About El Salvador," *New York Times*, February 21, 1981.

[22] The insurgency would continue through 1990, despite Cuban encouragement for negotiations as early as 1982 and the ending of Soviet materiel support in 1988 (Álvarez, 2010, pp. 29–30). In 1990, despite a decade of war, the FMLN had not "suffered the significant defeats, the large-scale defections, the weakening of their rural support, and the increase in active support for the government and armed forces of El Salvador that would signal the insurgency's decline" (Benjamin C. Schwarz, *American Counterinsurgency Doctrine and El Salvador: The Frustrations of Reform and the Illusions of Nation Building*, Santa Monica, Calif.: RAND Corporation, R-4042-USDP, 1991, p. 3).

[23] These conditions were as follows: "eliminating the repressive state apparatus, such as paramilitary groups; reforming and vetting the armed forces; building a new National Civilian Police; approving constitutional and judicial reforms; and reforming the electoral system, which included legalizing the FMLN as a political party"

judicial and party system and a structural transformation of the entire security sector. These reforms reshaped the police, intelligence services, and armed forces.[24]

Linking structural reforms to other security arrangements ultimately proved effective in El Salvador. FMLN fighters demobilized and began the slow process of reintegration. As a formal political party, the FMLN competed in its first elections in 1994. While some groups would eventually split from the party, forming their own electoral blocs, the FMLN effectively transitioned from an insurgent group to a regular political organization. By 2000, the FMLN had become the most powerful organization in El Salvador's Legislative Assembly and held the presidency from 2009 to 2019.[25]

Kosovo: Kosovo Liberation Army

The KLA was a militia force that formed in the mid-1990s to fight for Kosovo's independence from Yugoslavia. Drawing on support from the Albanian diaspora, the KLA tapped into unmet demands for Kosovar independence.[26] Initially, the KLA formed around a small leadership core. As the group expanded over time, it drew on a diverse mix of foreign fighters and mercenaries from across Europe and the Middle East.[27] After other groups failed to deliver progress through more-peaceful means, the KLA began a series of attacks against Serb civilians and security forces.[28]

In 1999, the United Nations resolution that ended the conflict in Kosovo required the withdrawal of Serbian forces and the demilitarization of Kosovar combatant groups.[29] By the time international forces arrived in Kosovo, the KLA had already established itself as both a political and security presence throughout the country.[30] This presence gave its leadership leverage in negotiations. The KLA found ways to institutionalize its fighters. While some fighters joined the insurgency in Macedonia, others were absorbed into two newly built security institutions. The first was the

---

(Alexander Segovia, *Transitional Justice and DDR: The Case of El Salvador*, New York: International Center for Transitional Justice, June 2009, p. 1).

[24] Cate Buchanan and Joaquin Chavez, *Negotiating Disarmament: Guns and Violence in the El Salvador Peace Negotiations*, Geneva, Switzerland: Centre for Humanitarian Dialogue, March 2008.

[25] Álvarez, 2010, p. 7.

[26] Henry H. Perritt Jr., *Kosovo Liberation Army: The Inside Story of an Insurgency*, Champaign, Ill.: University of Illinois Press, 2008.

[27] John Pike, "Kosovo Liberation Army [KLA]," webpage, GlobalSecurity, undated.

[28] R. Cody Phillips, *Operation Joint Guardian: The U.S. Army in Kosovo*, Washington, D.C.: U.S. Army Center of Military History, 2007.

[29] United Nations Security Council, Resolution 1244, S/RES/1244 (1999), June 10, 1999.

[30] Nathalie Duclos, "The DDR in Kosovo: Collision and Collusion Among International Administrators and Combatants," *Peacebuilding*, Vol. 4, No. 1, 2016.

Kosovo Protection Corps (KPC), an unarmed civilian security agency that drew heavily from the ranks of the KLA. The second was the Kosovo Police, which also absorbed many former KLA members. Ex-combatants constituted approximately 40 percent of the new police force, which was fielded slowly over several years and monitored closely by UN Civilian Police.[31]

This DDR process achieved several practical objectives, but former KLA leaders retain significant influence in the government. The KPC and police were intended to meet the demands of many ex-fighters, who were uninterested in reintegrating into civilian life.[32] For some of the leaders, incorporation into political structures was an attractive alternative to militant life. Several key figures in the KLA made the transition to political life and became some of the most powerful political figures in the country. However, KLA leaders did not enter the political system as a single party or coherent bloc; instead, former commanders joined various parties across the political spectrum, diluting their influence and control over state institutions.

Practical success of the DDR program has not, however, relieved the international community of its enduring security burden in Kosovo. Residual ethnosectarian and political animosity and tensions with neighboring Serbia require the North Atlantic Treaty Organization to maintain a force of approximately 4,000 troops in Kosovo. These troops work with other partners, including the European Union's rule of law mission, to continue to set the conditions for long-term success.

Lebanon: Hezbollah

In the early 1980s, Hezbollah was just one of several militia groups promising to defend Lebanon's disenfranchised Shi'a community and to resist Israeli occupation.[33] Drawing on Iranian external support, Hezbollah consolidated its position and unified under a single command structure by the 1990s. After Israel's withdrawal from southern Lebanon in 2000, Hezbollah overran the Israeli-supported militias in the area and claimed victory over the occupation.[34]

Hezbollah later demonstrated its full capabilities in its 2006 war with Israel, which was broadly viewed as a political, if not military, victory for the militant group. What was once a parochial Shi'a militia was now seen by many Arabs as the only group

---

[31] Duclos, 2016.

[32] Ramadan Qehaja, Kosum Kosumi, and Florian Qehaja, "The Process of Demobilization and Integration of Former Kosovo Liberation Army Members—Kosovo's Perspective," Prishtina, Kosovo: Kosovar Center for Security Studies, April 2010.

[33] Augustus Richard Norton, *Hezbollah: A Short History*, Princeton, N.J.: Princeton University Press, 2009, pp. 32–33.

[34] "2000: Hezbollah Celebrates Israeli Retreat," BBC News, May 26, 2000.

that could defend Lebanon against Israel, which was widely perceived as the country's greatest threat.

In recent years, Hezbollah's political influence has grown as it increased its representation in parliament and wielded an effective veto on major policy issues.[35] And as of early 2021, Hezbollah is arguably the most powerful political and military group in Lebanon.

The window to demobilize Hezbollah—if it was ever open in the first place—has long since closed. DDR efforts in Lebanon have historically targeted smaller, more local militia groups. After the Ta'if Accord (conceived to end the civil war), Lebanon began a reintegration program in 1991, focusing on 50,000 former militia fighters. This effort also included a general amnesty for most militia groups, but it did not include Hezbollah's fighters, who refused to disarm.[36] Instead of confronting this growing challenge to civilian authority, the weak Lebanese government refused to push any tough political or security reforms that could upend the fragile peace. By allowing Hezbollah to effectively opt out of any meaningful DDR program, the government gave the militant group the space and freedom of movement to maintain (and further develop) a parallel military force distinct from the Lebanese Armed Forces (LAF).[37]

Having abandoned any hope of DDR, the United States and its allies have pursued an alternative strategy to undercut Hezbollah's influence in Lebanon: invest in the LAF and build its capabilities.[38] Security sector institution-building is a slow process that represents a multigenerational effort. Given Hezbollah's vast political influence and impressive military capabilities, the LAF cannot afford to challenge Hezbollah without unleashing a devastating civil war that it would almost certainly lose.[39] Arguably, none of the conditions necessary for successful DDR were (or are) evident in Lebanon vis-à-vis Hezbollah.

Three General Pathways for DDR Suggested by the Cases

Collectively, these five cases suggest three possible paths for Iraq and the PMF. None will fit exactly. Keep in mind that there are always alternatives to DDR for the armed

---

[35] Council on Foreign Relations, "Hezbollah (a.k.a. Hizbollah, Hizbu'llah)," background paper, August 13, 2008.

[36] Kari Karame, "Reintegration and the Relevance of Social Relations: The Case of Lebanon," *Conflict, Security and Development*, Vol. 9, No. 4, 2009, p. 496.

[37] Aram Nerguizian, "The Lebanese Armed Forces and Hezbollah: Military Dualism in Post-War Lebanon," Beirut, Lebanon: Carnegie Middle East Center, October 30, 2018.

[38] Richard Natonski and Thomas Trask, "US Has Given Lebanese Armed Forces a Pass with Hezbollah—Conditioning Aid Is Necessary," *The Hill*, July 5, 2019.

[39] Muni Katz and Nadav Pollak, *Hezbollah's Russian Military Education in Syria*, Washington, D.C.: Washington Institute for Near East Policy, December 24, 2015.

group: complete rejection of the government and a continuation of conflict or self-imposed isolation.

First Pathway: Integration and Cooption

The first such path might resemble that of Afghanistan's Northern Alliance and Kosovo's KLA. In both cases, fighters were folded into new or existing security institutions, while their leaders were coopted with prominent positions in the new government. This path reduces the militant threat while incorporating former commanders into elite institutions, which largely preserves the overall state structure and balance.

Second Pathway: Legitimate Political Competition

The second path may be more disruptive politically, as seen in the cases of the FMLN and UNITA. Demobilized fighters form a cohesive political party. Following this path, militant leaders transform their groups into effective party organizations that not only compete in but can win elections. Although an electoral threat to the incumbent government, they are no longer an existential threat to the state.

Third Pathway: Shared Sovereignty

Among our five case studies, the third path is unique to Hezbollah, but it is fairly common in other weak states where there are no third-party security guarantors.[40] In Lebanon, there was no real effort to demobilize and disarm Hezbollah fighters. In avoiding confrontation, successive Lebanese governments have allowed the problem to fester. Hezbollah has since become the single most powerful actor in Lebanon, having developed parallel governance and security institutions that threaten the state's legitimacy and its monopoly on violence.

Potential Political Ramifications of DDR

Collectively, these cases also suggest that, in the short term, the demobilization of fighters can be difficult unless linked to complementary political and structural reforms that provide greater inclusion in state institutions. Absent the political will and the patience to pursue long-term reform, state authorities and international actors tend to accept a compromise position that effectively incorporates fighters into existing secu-

---

[40] The term *shared sovereignty* is from Paul Staniland, although the Hezbollah example does not neatly fit into any of Staniland's six-part typology (Paul Staniland, "States, Insurgents, and Wartime Political Orders," *Perspectives on Politics*, Vol. 10, No. 2, June 2012). We note that the general term *armed politics*, which "begins when an armed group emerges as a coherent actor and begins to interact with and/or make claims on the government," may perhaps better capture the Hezbollah example (Paul Staniland, "Armed Politics and the Study of Intrastate Conflict," *Journal of Peace Research*, Vol. 54, No. 4, 2017, p. 460). We thank Steve Watts for this critical observation.

rity institutions without first addressing the underlying structural problems endemic to those systems. In Afghanistan, Northern Alliance fighters initially resisted demobilization, but many were eventually folded into the Ministry of Interior and Afghan Army, as were some of UNITA's fighters in Angola. Large numbers of KLA members joined Kosovo's civilian police and emergency response agencies, while the group's leaders retained some influence over their former fighters in the government's security services. Importantly, in both Kosovo and Afghanistan, there was a capable international force presence encouraging DDR and contributing to local security.

For domestic political actors, the consequence of this approach—which does provide some respite from conflict—is that it may create political competition. While international stakeholders may be willing to accept this trade-off, it can be a harder sell for domestic actors.

In most of our cases, former militant leaders would later wield considerable influence through formal state institutions. UNITA is now (as of early 2021) the largest opposition party to the government. Former commanders from the Northern Alliance and KLA have left the militant groups behind to become political elites in their post-conflict governments. One could argue that the success of the FMLN in obtaining negotiated concessions, coupled with its subsequent political victories, made the Salvadoran DDR process a strategic success for the insurgents. Alternatively, one could argue that the FMLN case represents programmatic DDR success: A weak but legitimate democratic process evolved from a violent conflict. Both arguments appear to be true. This case suggests that the tactical, practical aspects of reintegration do not necessarily convey government success.

The implication for Iraq and future U.S. interests in Iraq is that even successful DDR might leave PMF leaders—and their Iranian backers—politically empowered, with legitimate voices in government.

CHAPTER FOUR

Considering DDR and Policy Alternatives in Iraq

Given the limits of U.S. influence in Iraq, the United States may have little say in the specific DDR policy or program design. However, ignoring the PMF or allowing them to increase their influence within Iraq's security services and political bodies may harm Iraqi democracy and undermine U.S. and allied strategic interests in Iraq and the greater Middle East. Given these stakes, it is critical that the United States and its allies find ways to limit the political influence of the PMF.

Our historical analysis indicates that DDR focused on the PMF will be extremely difficult unless linked to complementary SSR and political reforms that provide greater inclusion. Further, DDR programming pushed by the United States is anticipated to be particularly problematic and likely to backfire. Pressure from American leaders against the PMF would give Iranian-backed PMF leaders a rallying cry to regain some of their dwindling prestige and to divert some negative attention away from Iran. Direct U.S. intervention would also shift negative public attention in Iraq from the PMF to the United States, further undermining American influence. While reducing Iranian-backed PMF power and influence might be beneficial to the United States, a policy that seeks to force that reduction might, in fact, have the opposite effect.

Lessons for Iraq from the Historical Cases

Our case study analysis suggests that DDR programs can help support post-conflict stabilization efforts, but that enduring success often depends on complementary structural reforms and compliant partners. Groups that see no direct benefit in joining the political process *and* are able to sustain themselves with self-generated income or external sponsorship are unlikely to submit to DDR in any meaningful way.

Angola's series of failed DDR efforts throughout the 1990s illustrate how this process critically depends on buy-in from the militant group. UNITA never really committed to the DDR process until leadership defections and military defeat weakened the group to the point that it had to accept the state's terms and negotiate peace. The case of El Salvador offers an alternative but no less informative lesson: The FMLN's position was strong enough that the group agreed to demobilize only on the condition that the government implement a series of reforms specified in the peace accord.

Getting buy-in from militant groups—either because they have few alternatives, as in the case of UNITA, or because the deal offers broader political concessions, as in the case of the FMLN—is critical to DDR success. Otherwise, militant groups may instead cherry-pick the most favorable opportunities for participation while submitting to few of the restrictions that the state would ideally impose. It is not a process that can be forced on unwilling groups, at least not without dangerous long-term consequences, as Lebanese politicians clearly feared in the early 1990s when they instead chose to ignore the growing problem of Hezbollah.

Nor does DDR always produce desired results when former combatants whose interests are at odds with those of the government are normalized in the post-conflict system. Under such conditions, the erstwhile militant opposition may eventually become the ruling regime, which can result in untold future problems for the international community.

American-Supported DDR in Iraq Is Not Currently Viable

Simply put, the conditions that favor DDR success, as seen in our case studies, do not hold for Iraq today. In early 2021, barring an unexpected paradigm shift in both the situation in Iraq and American influence,[1] neither the Iraqi government nor the U.S.-led coalition is in a position to implement a DDR policy toward the PMF.[2] Without broad support and buy-in from the Iraqi political establishment, pushing DDR would require that the United States publicly pressure the Iraqi government, accompanied by various enticements and threats. Such an approach could lead to increased instability, given that the PMF have already demonstrated their willingness to contest U.S. influence, and be counterproductive. There are at least five compelling reasons why pushing such a DDR effort is unlikely to succeed today.

The PMF May Be the Strongest Military Force in Iraq
Given the drawdown of U.S. and coalition forces, the ongoing challenges with the Iraqi Army and Federal Police, and the limited size of the CTS, the confederated militia groups of the PMF might be the most powerful single military force in Iraq.

---

[1] For more on American influence in Iraq, see Ben Connable, James Dobbins, Howard J. Shatz, Raphael S. Cohen, and Becca Wasser, *Weighing U.S. Troop Withdrawal from Iraq: Strategic Risks and Recommendations*, Santa Monica, Calif.: RAND Corporation, PE-362-OSD, 2020.

[2] Michael Knights, Hamdi Malik, and Aymenn Jawad Al-Tamimi, "The Future of Iraq's Popular Mobilization Forces," Washington, D.C.: Washington Institute for Near East Policy, May 28, 2020; Eli Manaker, "This Time Is Different: Can Iraq Rein in the PMF?" *Georgetown Security Studies Review*, Georgetown University Center for Security Studies, October 2, 2020.

Military strength incentivizes the PMF to remain under arms and in their current uniforms rather than to trade both for uncertain futures in the standing Iraqi security services or in civilian life.

The PMF Have Significant Political Influence

The Iraqi parliament is deeply divided, and PMF militia leaders have assumed influential positions in government, arguably giving them effective veto power over ministerial decisionmaking. Iranian-backed PMF units, operating under the de jure legal umbrella of the Iraqi government, exercise de facto security control over large portions of Iraq's population.[3] A comprehensive DDR program would be met with political pushback and, as we saw in the January 2020 vote to remove foreign military forces from Iraq, direct and effective threats against Iraqi politicians who might support the U.S. policy.

Civilian Workforce Alternatives Are Limited and Unattractive

Poor job prospects and the government's failure to equitably provide economic opportunities make alternatives to militia service unattractive.[4] In general, current militiamen can either depart and hope for the best in a difficult job market, or they can join the Army or Federal Police, in which they will have less power, worse equipment, and perhaps less pay.[5] In this, the experience of the Sons of Iraq program offers a cautionary tale to PMF personnel who might be willing to demobilize, because the Iraqi government failed to either find civilian jobs for members of the Sons of Iraq or effectively integrate them into the formal security forces.[6]

U.S. Influence Has Waned

As of early 2021, American influence over Iraqi policymakers is limited by countervailing Iranian influence and by the sharp decrease in American presence and invest-

---

[3]   In addition to previously cited sources on PMF influence and control, see John Davison, "Iraqi Shi'ite Groups Deepen Control in Strategic Sunni Areas," Reuters, June 13, 2019; and Tamer El-Ghobashy and Mustafa Salim, "As Iraq's Shiite Militias Expand Their Reach, Concerns About an ISIS Revival Grow," *Washington Post*, January 9, 2019.

[4]   Helena Skinner, "Why Iraqis Are Protesting After 'Years of Anger and Frustration,'" *EuroNews*, April 10, 2019; European Asylum Support Office, *Country of Origin Information Report: Iraq Security Situation*, Brussels, Belgium, March 2019.

[5]   They would also lose the hard-won camaraderie that they have developed with their fellow militiamen in the fight against the Islamic State, and they would have to abandon their primary identity groups. For more on the value of camaraderie and principal identities, see Ben Connable, Michael J. McNerney, William Marcellino, Aaron Frank, Henry Hargrove, Marek N. Posard, S. Rebecca Zimmerman, Natasha Lander, Jasen J. Castillo, and James Sladden, *Will to Fight: Analyzing, Modeling, and Simulating the Will to Fight of Military Units*, Santa Monica, Calif.: RAND Corporation, RR-2341-A, 2018, Chapter Two.

[6]   Peterson, 2014; Al-Nidawi and Knights, 2018.

ment in Iraq during the 2003–2011 period.[7] Iraq is a sovereign state with a challenged but functioning political process: Iraqi politicians no longer respond to an American proconsul as they did in 2003. American diplomats and political leaders can apply leverage to influence Iraqi policies, but they cannot dictate Iraqi policy. Therefore, (1) *imposing* a DDR policy is not possible, and (2) the requisite diplomatic leverage to *influence* a DDR policy is lacking.

In this, the KLA (Kosovo) and Northern Alliance (Afghanistan) offer a critical lesson. Both agreed to disband because they had already established a strong political position and there was a friendly and capable international military presence that was urging demobilization and offering to assure security. The PMF have also established a strong political position. But the PMF perceive the international force now in Iraq— that is, the United States—as neither friendly nor capable enough, given its limited size, to fill the security gap left by a PMF disbandment.

Meddling in Iraqi Politics Is Likely to Backfire

Any public attempt by American policymakers to push a DDR policy on the Iraqi government or to pursue the dismantling of the PMF would have a high likelihood of backfiring. In early 2021, the United States and its policies in Iraq are a relatively minor public consideration. Civilians are primarily concerned with malign Iranian influence and Iraqi government corruption.[8] While the PMF has worn out its welcome in many areas—many groups are increasingly abusive in the face of street protests— the organization still has the support of many Shi'a Arabs who arguably make up the majority of the Iraqi population.[9]

Asserting a policy to dismantle the PMF would almost certainly shift negative attention toward the United States and its allies. Pressure from American leaders against the PMF would give Iranian-backed PMF leaders a rallying cry to regain some of their gradually dwindling prestige and divert some negative attention from Iran. While reducing Iranian-backed PMF power and influence might be beneficial to the United States, a policy that seeks to force that reduction might, in fact, have the opposite effect.

Policymakers should also be wary of implementing nonovert programs to undermine the PMF, including seemingly low-risk, backdoor diplomatic entreaties. Very little that the United States does in Iraq escapes public attention. Pursuing what might

---

[7]   For more on reduced U.S. influence in Iraq, see, for example, Douglas A. Ollivant, "A New Source of U.S. Influence in Iraq," *Lawfare*, August 11, 2019; and Michael Rubin, "How the United States Could Lose Iraq," *National Interest*, September 21, 2019.

[8]   For more on Iraqi perceptions in 2019, see National Democratic Institute, *Iraq Post-Daesh: Improved Social Cohesion, but Iraqis Remain Dissatisfied with Government*, national survey findings, Washington, D.C.: National Democratic Institute, July 2019.

[9]   For more on the relative power and popularity of the PMF, see Renad Mansour, "More Than Militias: Iraq's Popular Mobilization Forces Are Here to Stay," *War on the Rocks*, April 3, 2018.

be considered low-visibility efforts to generate a DDR policy against the PMF might actually increase the likelihood of blowback.

Concluding Thoughts

While this analysis of existing cases suggests that U.S.-backed DDR has a low chance of success in Iraq, the cost of taking no action may also be high. Two RAND reports published in 2020—*An Enduring American Commitment in Iraq: Shaping a Long-Term Strategy with Iraqi Army Partners* and *Weighing U.S. Troop Withdrawal from Iraq: Strategic Risks and Recommendations*—offer a broader perspective and specific recommendations for U.S. policy.[10]

---

[10] Connable, 2020a; Connable et al., 2020.

Details on 30 Case Studies

Table A.1 provides a brief summary of DDR efforts and details the references that were used for the 30 cases discussed in Chapter Two. The coding of PMF-related characteristics and three core outcomes are based on this text and the document or documents referenced in each. For additional details on the five case studies that are the focus of Chapter Three, we direct the reader to the more detailed discussions provided in that chapter.

Table A.1
Coded Analysis of 30 Existing DDR Cases

Case Number	Country	Group	Description and Sourcing
1	Afghanistan	Northern Alliance	See Chapter Three.
2	—	Taliban	The Taliban was de facto excluded from initial DDR programs in the wake of its defeat, and DDR programs specifically targeting it were not established until 2005. These programs consistently excluded senior Taliban leaders, and the lack of any type of peace process with the Taliban is credited as significantly limiting their efficacy (Derksen, 2015).
3–5	Angola	UNITA	See Chapter Three.
6	Bosnia	ARBiH	The Army of the Republic of Bosnia and Herzegovina (in Bosnian, Armija Republike Bosne i Hercegovine or ARBiH), also referred to as the Territorial Defence Force of the Republic of Bosnia and Hercegovina, was the official military force of the government of Bosnia and Herzegovina formed in 1992 to defend against the Army of Republika Srpska (VRS) that had put the capital of Sarajevo under siege in April 1992. The ARBiH, a Bosniak (Bosnian-Muslim) force, signed a ceasefire with the Croatian Defence Council (HVO) in 1994, and together they established the Armed Forces of Bosnia and Herzegovina (AFBiH). The AFBiH became the security force of the newly forming Bosniak-Croat enclave, although the vast majority of fighters (unofficially) demobilized in the wake of the Dayton Peace Accords (DPA) (Pietz, 2004, p. 25). This force received U.S.-funded security assistance for six years, beginning in 1996, "to balance Serb military advantages, to sever Muslim-Bosniac cooperation with Iran, and to foster Muslim-Croat military integration" (Heinemann-Grüder, Pietz, and Duffy, 2003, p. 12). The Serbian enclave security forces would join the AFBiH to form a single national security force in 2006.

Table A.1—Continued

Case Number	Country	Group	Description and Sourcing
7	—	HVO	The Croatian Defence Council (in Croatian, Hrvatsko vijeće obrane or HVO) was the military wing of the Croatian Democratic Union, the Bosnian Croat political party. In 1992, the HVO absorbed the fighters from the Croatian Defense Force (HOS), a Muslim-Croat force aligned with another Croatian political party— all Muslim fighters were disarmed and expelled (Bjelakovic and Strazzari, 1999, p. 85). In 1994, the HVO combined with the ARBiH to form the AFBiH and their trajectory follows that described for the ARBiH immediately above (Bjelakovic and Strazzari, 1999, pp. 73–102).
8	—	VRS	In 1992, a majority of Bosnians (nearly 100 percent) voted for independence from Yugoslavia in a referendum that was boycotted by Bosnian Serbs. The Bosnian Serbs seized more than two-thirds of the territory of Bosnia and advocated for unification with Serbia (Garding, 2019, p. 2). The Bosnian Serb Army (in Serbian, Vojska Republike Srpske or VRS) became the military army of the "state" established by Bosnian Serbs (Republika Srpska) in this territory. Supported by paramilitary and conventional units from Serbia, the VRS participated (along with its two primary antagonists) in what has been widely described as "ethnic cleansing" as it sought to "purify" land that it sought to claim (Garding, 2019, p. 3). Following the DPA, the leadership of the VRS became the leadership of the Serbian enclave formalized by the DPA (Moratti and Sabic-El-Rayess, 2009, p. 9) and the fighters became the security force for that enclave. The DPA did not contain any specific targets for the demobilization of forces, and the vast majority of VRS fighters simply disappeared in the following days (Pietz, 2004, p. 25). Over the next decade, the size of the Serbian armed forces decreased substantially before they were consolidated (in 2006) into today's single Armed Forces of Bosnia and Herzegovina (Garding, 2019; Pietz, 2004; Moratti and Sabic-El-Rayess, 2009).
9	Burundi	Tutsi militias	In the wake of a Tutsi coup against the recently elected Hutu president, Tutsi "self-defense groups" targeted Hutu civilians between 1993 and 1996. In 1996, Major Pierre Buyoya (a Tutsi) seized power and demobilized these militias by integrating them into the armed forces (Human Rights Watch, 2001, p. 4).
10	—	Hutu groups	In 1993, following the election of a Hutu as president in the first democratic election in Burundi's history, Tutsi military officers led a coup that culminated in the assassination of the president and the establishment of a military government. Over the next decade, the predominantly Tutsi military fought the Hutu Conseil National pour la Défense de la Démocratie–Forces de Défense de la Démocratie (CNDD-FDD). The CNDD-FDD agreed to a ceasefire in 2002, a Hutu from the CNDD-FDD was elected to the presidency in 2005, and the last remaining rebel group agreed to a ceasefire in 2006 (Fuhlrott, 2007, p. 325). Ex-combatants were either integrated into a newly established army or provided a stipend and demobilized (Fuhlrott, 2007, p. 326).

Table A.1—Continued

Case Number	Country	Group	Description and Sourcing
11	Cambodia	Khmer Rouge	The Khmer Rouge were excluded from initial DDR efforts and fought an insurgency against the government before finally surrendering completely in 1999. Beginning in 1996, following a royal amnesty, Khmer Rouge elements began to be absorbed into the national armed forces. Then, beginning in 1999, the armed forces shed roughly one-third of their personnel over a three-year period (Ferry, 2014, pp. 132, 139–141).
12	—	FUNCINPEC	The former king of Cambodia formed FUNCINPEC (acronym based on the French) in 1982 to contest a Vietnamese-supported government that had taken power in 1979. Following a 1991 ceasefire, FUNCINPEC became part of the new government. The military elements of FUNCINPEC were integrated in their entirety into the new state's security system (Ferry, 2014, p. 138). Complete disarmament was resisted because these forces were seen as a critical counter to the continued threat from the Khmer Rouge (Bartu and Wilford, 2009, p. 9).
13	Djibouti	FRUD	The Front for the Restoration of Unity and Democracy (FRUD) was established as a coalition of disparate resistance parties (Abdallah, 2007, p. 276), largely aligned with Djibouti's Afar minority (Berhe and Adaye, 2007, p. 4). The FRUD split following a French-brokered peace agreement; FRUD officials were given ministerial positions, and "some FRUD combatants were integrated into the Djiboutian army" (Berhes and Adaye, 2007, p. 4). A splinter element refused to participate in the new government but later made peace with it (Berhe and Adaye, 2007; Abdallah, 2007).
14	El Salvador	FMLN	See Chapter Three.
15	Ethiopia	Derg	The Derg, a communist military government that had been supported by the Soviet Union, ruled Ethiopia from 1974 to 1991. It was defeated by the Ethiopian People's Revolutionary Democratic Front (EPRDF) in 1991, and some 250,000 soldiers of the defeated Derg army volunteered for demobilization (Berhe, 2017).
16	—	EPRDF	The Ethiopian People's Revolutionary Democratic Front (EPRDF) defeated the existing communist military government in 1991, with the EPRDF army becoming the new national army (Berhe, 2017, p. 169). Some 150,000 were demobilized after the end of a war with Eritrea (Berhe, 2017, p. 173).
17	Kosovo	KLA	See Chapter Three.
18	Lebanon	Hezbollah	See Chapter Three.
19	Namibia	PLAN	The People's Liberation Army of Namibia (PLAN) was the military wing of the South-West Africa People's Organization that fought against South Africa for independence during the 1966–1989 Namibian War for Independence. With Angolan, Cuban, and Soviet support, PLAN sustained a 27-year campaign against South African forces. Following the peace accords, about 20 percent of PLAN military forces were integrated into the newly forming Namibian security forces, while the remaining 80 percent were provided no integration plan, as the "powerful political imperatives of national reconciliation and nation building" were prioritized over reintegration (Dzinesa, 2006, p. 263).

Table A.1—Continued

Case Number	Country	Group	Description and Sourcing
20	—	SWATF	The South West Africa Territorial Force (SWATF) was a South African–trained Namibian counterinsurgency force, initially formed in 1974, that supported the South African Defense Force during the Namibian War of Independence (U.S. Central Intelligence Agency, 1982). The United Nations Transition Assistance Group, which was formed after the 1988 peace accord, demobilized the SWATF in 1989. South Africa initially used elements of SWATF's sister force (the paramilitary Koevoet) to infiltrate the police to carry out punitive attacks against the PLAN, although they too were demobilized at the end of 1989 (Dzinesa, 2006, pp. 262–263).
21	Nepal	Maoists	Following a ten-year insurgency, the relatively small Maoist insurgency (around 20,000 fighters) was demobilized and placed in cantonments. In 2012, the fighters were released from the cantonments with a relatively small number (about 10 percent) joining the Nepali Army and the vast majority accepting a cash-based retirement stipend paid directly by Nepal (Bhandari, 2015, pp. 65–66).
22	Nicaragua	Contras	The Contras, a guerilla movement that received significant U.S. support, fought a decade-long rural insurgency against the socialist Sandinista government. In 1990, after seven years of negotiations and a Sandinista loss at the ballot box in February 1990, the Contras signed a peace accord with the new U.S-supported government and the Sandinista Army that would provide them cash, plots of land, and representation in the government in exchange for demobilization (Khokhar, 2008, pp. 61–63). The withdrawal of U.S. support for the Contras is credited as playing a key role in the success of the peace agreement and their willingness to negotiate (Khokhar, 2008, p. 56). Once the process began, the Contras demobilized and disarmed very rapidly over a five-month period (Khokhar, 2008, p. 88).
23	Papua New Guinea	BRA and BRF	The Bougainville Revolutionary Army (BRA) formed in 1988, seeking independence from Papua New Guinea following protracted tensions attributed to the arrival of large numbers of both immigrants and migrants from elsewhere in Papua New Guinea after the establishment of a major copper mine on Bougainville Island in 1972. Fighting between the BRA and Papua New Guinea lasted for a decade, with government forces using the Bougainville Resistance Forces (BRF) as a local proxy. Following a New Zealand–brokered peace agreement between the BRA and BRF in 1997, a multinational peacekeeping force began what would be a six-year peacekeeping operation (1997–2003) in Bougainville (Reddy, 2008, pp. 121–122). The Bougainville Peace Agreement in 2001 formally ended the war, creating a path to independence for Bougainville and establishing a plan for weapons disposal (Bohane, 2019). Though 80 percent of BRA and BRF weapons were destroyed by 2004 (UNIFEM, 2004, p. 26), with fighters given development projects (UNIFEM, 2004, pp. 26–29), several groups still maintain control of their weapons as insurance against the Papua New Guinea government (Bohane, 2019).

Table A.1—Continued

Case Number	Country	Group	Description and Sourcing
24	Tajikistan	UTO	The United Tajik Opposition (UTO) was a compilation of groups that wanted either "democratic reforms or Islamic renewal" in Tajikistan in the wake of the collapse of the Soviet Union (Torjesen and MacFarlane, 2007, p. 314). Supported financially by the Middle East and by Tajik ethnic enclaves in Afghanistan, the UTO signed an agreement with the existing government that gave the UTO representation in the government, and UTO military elements were absorbed as units into the armed forces (Torjesen and MacFarlane, pp. 314 and 316).
25	Uganda	UNLA	The Uganda National Liberation Army (UNLA) was the military force that, alongside Tanzanian forces, defeated then-President Idi Amin. The UNLA was defeated by the National Resistance Army (NRA) in 1986, following a six-year insurgency, and subsequently fled into northern Uganda and the Sudan. After a two-year insurgency, former UNLA leaders and the NRA signed a peace accord, granting amnesty to up to 10,000 UNLA fighters and absorbing many of these fighters into the NRA (Day, 2011, pp. 448–449).
26	—	NRA	The National Resistance Army (NRA) was the victor of the six-year (1980–1986) Uganda Bush War, allowing the National Resistance Movement (an alliance of the Popular Resistance Army and Uganda Freedom Fighters) to establish a new government in 1986. Demobilization of the NRA occurred from 1992 to 1995 after open rebellion against the new government was quelled in 1991 (Colletta, Kostner, and Wiederhofer, 1996, p. 219). Approximately one-third of the NRA's 90,000 fighters were demobilized and provided financial resources to comply, with the remaining fighters used to form the Uganda People's Defence Force when a constitution was enacted (Colletta, Kostner, and Wiederhofer, 1996, p. 219).
27	—	UA, FUNA, UNRF	The Uganda Army (UA), Former Uganda National Army (FUNA), and Uganda National Rescue Front (UNRF) were constituted from elements of Amin's army (defeated in 1979). The UA, FUNA, and UNRF fought against the UNLA from 1980 to 1985, although only the UNRF was absorbed into the NRA, while the UA and FUNA "dissolved into Sudan and Congo" (Day, 2011, p. 451).
28	—	WNBF, UNRF II	The Uganda National Rescue Front II (UNRF II) and West Nile Bank Front (WNBF) formed in the mid-1990s from Amin-era military elements and became part of a Sudan-led campaign against the NRA beginning in 1994. Both were absorbed into the NRA during the 1997–2002 time frame (Day, 2011, pp. 451–452).

Table A.1—Continued

Case Number	Country	Group	Description and Sourcing
29	—	LRA	The Lord's Resistance Army (LRA) emerged from the resistance, beginning in 1986, against targeted attacks on the Acholi being prosecuted by Ugandan government forces. With a force of only "200 or 300" willing volunteers—and tens of thousands of others who had been forcibly recruited—Joseph Kony led the LRA in a 20-year (1987–2006) rebellion that led to an estimated 100,000 deaths (Osborne, 2019). International nongovernmental organizations have supported the reintegration of LRA inductees into their communities since 1994, and in 2002, after the passing of a blanket amnesty for LRA fighters, a unit within the Uganda People's Defence Force was set up to provide another reintegration opportunity for LRA fighters and eventually grew in strength to nearly 1,000 (Borzello, 2007, pp. 398 and 405). This unit, 105 Battalion, was used to track the LRA until 2015, when the 105 was decommissioned (Easter and Hatangimana, 2017, p. 26). In 2008, after two years of peace talks failed, Kony fled with his remaining LRA forces into the Democratic Republic of the Congo (Easter and Hatangimana, 2017, p. 34).
30	Zimbabwe	RSF, ZANLA, ZIPRA	The 1964–1979 Rhodesian Bush War, in which the Zimbabwe African National Liberation Army (ZANLA) and Zimbabwe People's Revolutionary Army (ZIPRA) contested the Rhodesian Security Forces (RSF), concluded with the signing of the Lancaster House Agreement. The agreement did not discuss DDR, and the newly forming government integrated the three warring parties into a new national army (Dzinesa, 2006, p. 258).

Abbreviations

AFBiH	Armed Forces of Bosnia and Herzegovina
ARBiH	Army of the Republic of Bosnia and Herzegovina
BRA	Bougainville Revolutionary Army
BRF	Bougainville Resistance Forces
CNDD-FDD	Conseil National pour la Défense de la Démocratie–Forces de Défense de la Démocratie
CTS	Counter-Terrorism Service
DDR	disarmament, demobilization, and reintegration
DPA	Dayton Peace Accords
EPRDF	Ethiopian People's Revolutionary Democratic Front
FMLN	Farabundo Martí National Liberation Front
FRUD	Front for the Restoration of Unity and Democracy
FUNA	Former Uganda National Army
FUNCINPEC	National United Front for an Independent, Neutral, Peaceful and Cooperative Cambodia
HOS	Croatian Defense Force
HVO	Croatian Defense Council
KLA	Kosovo Liberation Army
KPC	Kosovo Protection Corps
LAF	Lebanese Armed Forces
LRA	Lord's Resistance Army
NRA	National Resistance Army
PLAN	People's Liberation Army of Namibia
PMF	Popular Mobilization Forces
RSF	Rhodesian Security Forces
SSR	security sector reform

SWATF	South West Africa Territorial Force
TMF	tribal militia force
UA	Uganda Army
UN	United Nations
UNIFEM	United Nations Development Fund for Women
UNITA	National Union for the Total Independence of Angola
UNLA	Uganda National Liberation Army
UNRF	Uganda National Rescue Front
UNRF II	Uganda National Rescue Front II
UTO	United Tajik Opposition
VRS	Vojska Republike Srpske (Bosnian Serb Army)
WNBF	West Nile Bank Front
ZANLA	Zimbabwe African National Liberation Army
ZIPRA	Zimbabwe People's Revolutionary Army

References

"2000: Hezbollah Celebrates Israeli Retreat," BBC News, May 26, 2000. As of April 27, 2021:
http://news.bbc.co.uk/onthisday/hi/dates/stories/may/26/newsid_2496000/2496423.stm

Abdallah, Abdo A., "State Building, Independence and Post-Conflict Reconstruction in Djibouti,"
in Ulf Johansson Dahre, ed., *Post-Conflict Peace-Building in the Horn of Africa: A Report of the 6th
Annual Conference on the Horn of Africa, Lund, August 24–26, 2007*, Lund, Sweden: Lund University
Department of Political Science, 2007, pp. 269–279. As of December 2, 2019:
http://www.sirclund.se/Conference%20report%202007.pdf#page=269

Aboulenein, Ahmed, "Iraqi Rival Groups Both Announce Parliamentary Blocs to Form New
Government," Reuters, September 2, 2018. As of April 27, 2021:
https://www.reuters.com/article/us-iraq-politics/iraqi-rival-groups-both-announce-parliamentary-
blocs-to-form-new-government-idUSKCN1LI0SM

"After Soleimani and Muhandis, Pro-Iranian Factions in Iraq Are Weakened, Divided," *Arab Weekly*,
June 12, 2020. As of February 7, 2021:
https://thearabweekly.com/after-soleimani-and-muhandis-pro-iranian-factions-iraq-are-
weakened-divided

Al-Gabouri, Adel, *The Role of the Popular Mobilization Forces in the Iraqi Political Process*,
Washington, D.C.: Washington Institute for Near East Policy, October 1, 2019. As of April 27, 2021:
https://www.washingtoninstitute.org/fikraforum/view/the-role-of-the-popular-mobilization-forces-
in-the-iraqi-political-process

Al-Iraqi, Mohammad, "Iran and Armed Militias in Post-ISIS Iraq," *Journal for Iranian Studies*,
Vol. 1, No. 3, June 2017, pp. 96–115. As of April 27, 2021:
https://rasanah-iiis.org/english/wp-content/uploads/sites/2/2018/07/
Iran-and-Armed-Militias-in-post-ISIS-Iraq.pdf

Al-Nidawi, Omar, *The Growing Economic and Political Role of Iraq's PMF*, Washington, D.C.:
Middle East Institute, May 21, 2019. As of December 2, 2019:
https://www.mei.edu/publications/growing-economic-and-political-role-iraqs-pmf

Al-Nidawi, Omar, and Michael Knights, *Militias in Iraq's Security Forces: Historical Context and U.S.
Options*, Washington, D.C.: The Washington Institute for Near East Policy, February 22, 2018. As
of March 24, 2021:
https://www.washingtoninstitute.org/policy-analysis/militias-iraqs-security-forces-historical-context-
and-us-options

Alaaldin, Ranj, *Containing Shiite Militias: The Battle for Stability in Iraq*, Doha, Qatar: Brookings
Doha Center, 2017. As of April 27, 2021:
https://www.brookings.edu/wp-content/uploads/2017/12/12_17_shiite_militias_in_iraq.pdf

————, *What Will Happen to Iraqi Shiite Militias After One Key Leader's Death?* Washington, D.C.: Brookings Institution, March 3, 2020. As of February 7, 2021: https://www.brookings.edu/blog/order-from-chaos/2020/03/03/what-will-happen-to-iraqi-shiite-militias-after-one-key-leaders-death/

Álvarez, Alberto Martín, *From Revolutionary War to Democratic Revolution: The Farabundo Martí National Liberation Front (FMLN) in El Salvador*, Berlin, Germany: Berghof Conflict Research, Transitions Series No. 9, November 1, 2010. As of April 27, 2021: https://berghof-foundation.org/library/from-revolutionary-war-to-democratic-revolution-the-farabundo-mart%C3%AD-national-liberation-front-fmln-in-el-salvador

Atallah, Philippe, *The Future of the Iraqi Popular Mobilization Forces*, Philadelphia, Pa.: Foreign Policy Research Institute, August 19, 2019. As of April 27, 2021: https://www.fpri.org/article/2019/08/the-future-of-the-iraqi-popular-mobilization-forces/

Bartu, Peter, and Neil Wilford, *Transitional Justice and DDR: The Case of Cambodia*, New York: International Center for Transitional Justice, 2009. As of April 27, 2021: https://www.ictj.org/sites/default/files/ICTJ-DDR-Cambodia-CaseStudy-2009-English.pdf

Berhe, Mulugeta Gebrehiwot, "The Ethiopian Post-Transition Security Sector Reform Experience: Building a National Army from a Revolutionary Democratic Army," *African Security Review*, Vol. 26, No. 2, 2017, pp. 161–179.

Berhe, Tadesse, and Yonas Adaye, "Afar: The Impact of Local Conflict on Regional Stability," Pretoria, South Africa: Institute for Security Studies, 2007. As of April 27, 2021: https://www.files.ethz.ch/isn/123909/2007_05_01_Afar.pdf

Bhandari, Chiranjibi, "The Reintegration of Maoist Ex-Combatants in Nepal," *Economic and Political Weekly*, Vol. 50, No. 9, 2015, pp. 63–68.

Biddle, Stephen, "Victory Misunderstood: What the Gulf War Tells Us About the Future of Conflict," *International Security*, Vol. 21, No. 2, Fall 1996, pp. 139–179.

Bjelakovic, Nebojsa, and Francesco Strazzari, "The Sack of Mostar, 1992–1994: The Politico-Military Connection," *European Security*, Vol. 8, No. 2, Summer 1999, pp. 73–102.

Blanchard, Christopher M., *Iraq: Issues in the 116th Congress*, Washington, D.C.: Congressional Research Service, R45633, updated July 17, 2020.

Bohane, Ben, *The Bougainville Referendum and Beyond*, Australia Square, Australia: Lowy Institute, October 8, 2019. As of April 27, 2021: https://www.lowyinstitute.org/publications/bougainville-referendum-and-beyond#_ednref6

Borzello, Anna, "The Challenge of DDR in Northern Uganda: The Lord's Resistance Army," *Conflict, Security and Development*, Vol. 7, No. 3, 2007, pp. 387–415.

Buchanan, Cate, and Joaquin Chavez, *Negotiating Disarmament: Guns and Violence in the El Salvador Peace Negotiations*, Geneva, Switzerland: Centre for Humanitarian Dialogue, March 2008. As of April 27, 2021: https://gsdrc.org/document-library/negotiating-disarmament-guns-and-violence-in-the-el-salvador-peace-negotiations/

Clark, Kate, *Graft and Remilitarisation: A Look Back at Efforts to Disarm, Demobilise, Reconcile, and Reintegrate*, Kabul, Afghanistan: Afghanistan Analysts Network, July 12, 2018. As of April 27, 2021: https://www.afghanistan-analysts.org/graft-and-remilitarisation-a-look-back-at-efforts-to-disarm-demobilise-reconcile-and-reintegrate/

Colletta, Nat J., Markus Kostner, and Ingo Wiederhofer, *Case Studies in War-to-Peace Transition: The Demobilization and Reintegration of Ex-Combatants in Ethiopia, Namibia, and Uganda*, Washington, D.C.: World Bank, Discussion Paper No. 331, 1996. As of April 27, 2021:
https://gsdrc.org/document-library/war-to-peace-transition-the-demobilization-and-reintegration-of
-ex-combatants-in-uganda/

Connable, Ben, *An Enduring American Commitment in Iraq: Shaping a Long-Term Strategy with Iraqi Army Partners*, Santa Monica, Calif.: RAND Corporation, PE-353-OSD, 2020a. As of April 27, 2021:
https://www.rand.org/pubs/perspectives/PE353.html

———, "Iraq's Vote to Expel U.S. Troops Is Iran's True Victory," *Los Angeles Times*, January 5, 2020b.

Connable, Ben, James Dobbins, Howard J. Shatz, Raphael S. Cohen, and Becca Wasser, *Weighing U.S. Troop Withdrawal from Iraq: Strategic Risks and Recommendations*, Santa Monica, Calif.: RAND Corporation, PE-362-OSD, 2020. As of April 27, 2021:
https://www.rand.org/pubs/perspectives/PE362.html

Connable, Ben, Michael J. McNerney, William Marcellino, Aaron Frank, Henry Hargrove, Marek N. Posard, S. Rebecca Zimmerman, Natasha Lander, Jasen J. Castillo, and James Sladden, *Will to Fight: Analyzing, Modeling, and Simulating the Will to Fight of Military Units*, Santa Monica, Calif.: RAND Corporation, RR-2341-A, 2018. As of April 27, 2021:
https://www.rand.org/pubs/research_reports/RR2341.html

Cordesman, Anthony, and Abraham R. Wagner, *Lessons of Modern Warfare*, Vol. IV: *The Gulf War*, Boulder, Colo.: Westview Press, 1996.

Council on Foreign Relations, "Hezbollah (a.k.a. Hizbollah, Hizbu'llah)," background paper, August 13, 2008. As of April 27, 2021:
https://web.archive.org/web/20080913091527/http://www.cfr.org/publication/9155/hezbollah.
html?breadcrumb=%2F

Davison, John, "Iraqi Shi'ite Groups Deepen Control in Strategic Sunni Areas," Reuters, June 13, 2019. As of May 3, 2021:
https://www.reuters.com/article/us-iraq-militias-land-insight/iraqi-shiite-groups-deepen-control-
in-strategic-sunni-areas-idUSKCN1TE18D

Davison, John, and Ahmed Rasheed, "Fractures Grow Among Iraq Militias, Spell Political Retreat," Reuters, April 1, 2020. As of February 7, 2021:
https://www.reuters.com/article/us-iraq-militias/fractures-grow-among-iraq-militias-spell-politic
al-retreat-idUSKBN21J5EZ

Day, Christopher R., "The Fates of Rebels: Insurgencies in Uganda," *Comparative Politics*, Vol. 43, No. 4, July 2011, pp. 439–458.

Derksen, Deedee, *The Politics of Disarmament and Rearmament in Afghanistan*, Washington, D.C.: United States Institute of Peace, 2015. As of April 27, 2021:
https://www.usip.org/sites/default/files/PW110-The-Politics-of-Disarmament-and-Rearmament-in-
Afghanistan.pdf

Duclos, Nathalie, "The DDR in Kosovo: Collision and Collusion Among International Administrators and Combatants," *Peacebuilding*, Vol. 4, No. 1, 2016, pp. 41–53.

Dury-Agri, Jessa Rose, Omer Kassim, and Patrick Martin, *Iraqi Security Forces and Popular Mobilization Forces: Orders of Battle*, Washington, D.C.: Institute for the Study of War, December 2017. As of April 27, 2021:
http://www.understandingwar.org/report/iraqi-security-forces-and-popular-mobilization-forces-orders-battle-0

Dzinesa, Gwinyayi Albert, *Swords into Ploughshares—Disarmament, Demobilisation and Reintegration in Zimbabwe, Namibia and South Africa*, Pretoria, South Africa: Institute for Security Studies, ISS Paper 120, 2006. As of June 30, 2021:
https://www.files.ethz.ch/isn/98760/PAPER120.pdf

Easter, Jonathan R., and Benon M. Hatangimana, *Bending the Spear: The Campaign Against the Lord's Resistance Army*, thesis, Monterey, Calif.: Naval Postgraduate School, 2017. As of April 27, 2021:
https://apps.dtic.mil/dtic/tr/fulltext/u2/1053210.pdf

Eisenhammer, Stephen, "Angola's Ruling Party Declared Election Winner as Opposition Cries Foul," Reuters, August 25, 2017. As of April 27, 2021:
https://www.reuters.com/article/us-angola-election/angolas-ruling-party-declared-election-winner-as-opposition-cries-foul-idUSKCN1B5180

Eisenstadt, Michael, and Michael Knights, "Mini-Hizballahs, Revolutionary Guard Knock-Offs, and the Future of Iran's Militant Proxies in Iraq," *War on the Rocks*, May 9, 2017. As of April 27, 2021:
https://warontherocks.com/2017/05/mini-hizballahs-revolutionary-guard-knock-offs-and-the-future-of-irans-militant-proxies-in-iraq/

El-Ghobashy, Tamer, and Mustafa Salim, "As Iraq's Shiite Militias Expand Their Reach, Concerns About an ISIS Revival Grow," *Washington Post*, January 9, 2019.

European Asylum Support Office, *Country of Origin Information Report: Iraq Security Situation*, Brussels, Belgium, March 2019. As of April 28, 2021:
https://www.easo.europa.eu/sites/default/files/publications/EASO-COI-Report-Iraq-Security-situation.pdf

"Excerpts From Haig's Briefing About El Salvador," *New York Times*, February 21, 1981. As of April 27, 2021:
https://www.nytimes.com/1981/02/21/world/excerpts-from-haig-s-briefing-about-el-salvador.html?pagewanted=all

Felbab-Brown, Vanda, "Pitfalls of the Paramilitary Paradigm: The Iraqi State, Geopolitics, and Al-Hashd Al-Shaabi," policy brief, Washington, D.C.: Brookings Institution, June 2019. As of April 27, 2021:
https://www.brookings.edu/wp-content/uploads/2019/06/FP_20190625_iraq_felbab_brown.pdf

Ferry, Tiphaine, "How Disarmament, Demobilization and Reintegration Programs Could Have Facilitated the Establishment of Long-Term Conflict Prevention in Post-Conflict Cambodia," *Cambodia Law and Policy Journal*, Vol. 3, 2014, pp. 127–143. As of April 27, 2021:
http://cambodialpj.org/wp-content/uploads/2014/12/DCCAM_CLPJ_Ferry.pdf

Fuhlrott, Friederike, "Burundi After the Civil War: Demobilising and Reintegrating Ex-Combatants," *Africa Spectrum*, Vol. 42, No. 2, 2007, pp. 323–333.

Garding, Sarah E., *Bosnia and Herzegovina: Background and U.S. Policy*, Washington, D.C.: Congressional Research Service, R45691, April 15, 2019.

Gaston, Erica, and András Derzsi-Horváth, *Iraq After ISIL: Sub-State Actors, Local Forces, and the Micro-Politics of Control*, Berlin, Germany: Global Public Policy Institute, March 2018. As of April 27, 2021:
https://reliefweb.int/sites/reliefweb.int/files/resources/
Gaston_Derzsi-Horvath_2018_Iraq_After_ISIL.pdf

Hannah, John, "Iran-Backed Militias Are in Iraq to Stay," *Foreign Policy*, July 31, 2019. As of April 27, 2021:
https://foreignpolicy.com/2019/07/31/iran-backed-militias-are-in-iraq-to-stay/

Heinemann-Grüder, Andreas, Tobias Pietz, and Shay Duffy, *Turning Soldiers into a Work Force: Demobilization and Reintegration in Post-Dayton Bosnia and Herzegovina*, Bonn, Switzerland: Bonn International Center for Conversion, 2003. As of April 27, 2021:
https://www.bicc.de/uploads/tx_bicctools/brief27.pdf

Hiro, Dilip, *The Longest War: The Iran-Iraq Military Conflict*, London: Grafton Books, 1989.

Hosmer, Stephen T., *Why the Iraqi Resistance to the Coalition Invasion Was So Weak*, Santa Monica, Calif.: RAND Corporation, MG-544-AF, 2007. As of April 27, 2021:
https://www.rand.org/pubs/monographs/MG544.html

Human Rights Watch, *To Protect the People: The Government-Sponsored "Self-Defense" Program in Burundi*, New York, 2001. As of April 27, 2021:
https://www.hrw.org/reports/2001/burundi/burundi1201.pdf

"Iraqi Parliament Passes Contested Law on Shi'ite Paramilitaries," Reuters, November 26, 2016. As of April 27, 2021:
https://www.reuters.com/article/us-mideast-crisis-iraq-military/iraqi-parliament-passes-contested-law
-on-shiite-paramilitaries-idUSKBN13L0IE

"Iraq's Shi'ite Militias Formally Inducted into Security Forces," Reuters, March 8, 2018. As of April 27, 2021:
https://www.reuters.com/article/us-mideast-crisis-iraq-militias/iraqs-shiite-militias-formally-in
ducted-into-security-forces-idUSKCN1GK354

Jabar, Faleh A., "Chapter 6: The Iraqi Army and Anti-Army: Some Reflections on the Role of the Military," *Adelphi Papers*, Vol. 43, No. 354, 2003, pp. 115–130.

Johnson, Douglas M., *The Historical Foundations of World Order: The Tower and the Arena*, Leiden, Netherlands: Martinus Nijhoff Publishers, 2008.

Johnson, Rob, *The Iran-Iraq War*, London: Palgrave-Macmillan, 2011.

Karame, Kari, "Reintegration and the Relevance of Social Relations: The Case of Lebanon," *Conflict, Security and Development*, Vol. 9, No. 4, 2009, pp. 495–514. As of April 27, 2021:
https://www.tandfonline.com/doi/full/10.1080/14678800903345796

Katz, Muni, and Nadav Pollak, *Hezbollah's Russian Military Education in Syria*, Washington, D.C.: Washington Institute for Near East Policy, December 24, 2015. As of April 27, 2021:
https://www.washingtoninstitute.org/policy-analysis/view/
hezbollahs-russian-military-education-in-syria

Khokhar, Mariam, *The Dynamics of Demobilizing Under Friendly Governments: The Contras, The Paras, and DDR*, thesis, American University, Washington, D.C., 2008.

Knights, Michael, *The Long Haul: Rebooting U.S. Security Cooperation in Iraq*, Washington, D.C.: Washington Institute for Near East Policy, January 22, 2015.

———, *Popular Mobilization Force Reform in Iraq: Reintegration or Consolidation of Militia Power?* Washington, D.C.: Washington Institute for Near East Policy, July 8, 2019a. As of April 27, 2021: https://www.washingtoninstitute.org/policy-analysis/view/ popular-mobilization-force-reform-in-iraq-reintegration-or-consolidation-of

———, "Iran's Expanding Militia Army in Iraq: The New Special Groups," *CTC Sentinel*, Vol. 12, No. 7, August 2019b, pp. 1–12. As of April 27, 2021: https://ctc.usma.edu/app/uploads/2019/08/CTC-SENTINEL-072019.pdf

———, *Helping Iraq Take Charge of Its Command-and-Control Structure*, Washington, D.C.: Washington Institute for Near East Policy, September 30, 2019c. As of April 27, 2021: https://www.washingtoninstitute.org/policy-analysis/view/ helping-iraq-take-charge-of-its-command-and-control-structure

Knights, Michael, Hamdi Malik, and Aymenn Jawad Al-Tamimi, "The Future of Iraq's Popular Mobilization Forces," Washington, D.C.: Washington Institute for Near East Policy, May 28, 2020.

Malik, Hamdi, *The Future of Iraq's Popular Mobilization Forces*, Washington, D.C.: Carnegie Endowment for International Peace, September 21, 2017. As of April 27, 2021: https://carnegieendowment.org/sada/73186

Malovany, Pesach, *Wars of Modern Babylon: A History of the Iraqi Army from 1921 to 2003*, Lexington, Ky.: University Press of Kentucky, 2017.

Manaker, Eli, "This Time Is Different: Can Iraq Rein in the PMF?" *Georgetown Security Studies Review*, Georgetown University Center for Security Studies, October 2, 2020.

Mansour, Renad, "More Than Militias: Iraq's Popular Mobilization Forces Are Here to Stay," *War on the Rocks*, April 3, 2018. As of April 27, 2021: https://warontherocks.com/2018/04/more-than-militias-iraqs-popular-mobilization-forces- are-here-to-stay/

———, "Reining in Iraq's Paramilitaries Will Just Make Them Stronger," *Foreign Policy*, July 9, 2019. As of April 27, 2021: https://foreignpolicy.com/2019/07/09/reining-in-iraqs-paramilitaries-will-just-make-them-stronger/

McFate, Sean, "The Link Between DDR and SSR in Conflict-Affected Countries," Washington, D.C.: United States Institute of Peace, 2010.

Moratti, Massimo, and Amra Sabic-El-Rayess, *Transitional Justice and DDR: The Case of Bosnia and Herzegovina*, New York: International Center for Transitional Justice, 2009. As of April 27, 2021: https://www.ictj.org/sites/default/files/ICTJ-DDR-Bosnia-CaseStudy-2009-English.pdf

Murray, Williamson, and Kevin M. Woods, *The Iran-Iraq War: A Military and Strategic History*, Cambridge, UK: Cambridge University Press, 2014.

National Democratic Institute, *Iraq Post-Daesh: Improved Social Cohesion, but Iraqis Remain Dissatisfied with Government*, national survey findings, Washington, D.C.: National Democratic Institute, July 2019. As of April 28, 2021: https://www.ndi.org/sites/default/files/NDI%20Iraq%20Survey%202019_EN_0.pdf

Natonski, Richard, and Thomas Trask, "US Has Given Lebanese Armed Forces a Pass with Hezbollah—Conditioning Aid Is Necessary," *The Hill*, July 5, 2019. As of April 28, 2021: https://thehill.com/blogs/congress-blog/foreign-policy/ 451466-us-has-given-lebanese-armed-forces-a-pass-with-hezbollah

Nerguizian, Aram, "The Lebanese Armed Forces and Hezbollah: Military Dualism in Post-War Lebanon," Beirut, Lebanon: Carnegie Middle East Center, October 30, 2018. As of April 28, 2021:
https://carnegie-mec.org/2018/10/30/lebanese-armed-forces-and-hezbollah-military-dualism-in-post-war-lebanon-pub-77598

Norton, Augustus Richard, *Hezbollah: A Short History*, Princeton, N.J.: Princeton University Press, 2009.

O'Driscoll, Dylan, and Dave van Zoonen, "The Future of Iraq: Is Reintegration Possible?" *Middle East Policy*, Vol. 24, No. 3, Fall 2017, pp. 34–47.

Ollivant, Douglas A., "A New Source of U.S. Influence in Iraq," *Lawfare*, August 11, 2019. As of April 27, 2021:
https://www.lawfareblog.com/new-source-us-influence-iraq

Osborne, Matthew, "Truly Reconciled?" webpage, Stockholm Environment Institute, 2019. As of April 28, 2021:
https://www.sei.org/perspectives/truly-reconciled/

Pardew, James W., Jr., "The Iraqi Army's Defeat in Kuwait," *Parameters*, Vol. 21, No. 4, Winter 1991–1992, pp. 17–23.

Parry, Jacqueline, and Emily Burlinghaus, *Reintegration of Combatants in Iraq After ISIL*, Institute of Regional and International Studies, American University of Iraq, Sulaimani, April 2019. As of April 28, 2021:
https://auis.edu.krd/iris/sites/default/files/For%20WEB%20-%20Parry%20et%20al.pdf

Perritt, Henry H., Jr., *Kosovo Liberation Army: The Inside Story of an Insurgency*, Champaign, Ill.: University of Illinois Press, 2008.

Peterson, Scott, "Maliki or ISIS? Neither Looks Good to Sunni Awakening Veterans," *CSMonitor*, June 18, 2014. As of March 24, 2021:
https://www.csmonitor.com/World/Middle-East/2014/0618/Maliki-or-ISIS-Neither-looks-good-to-Sunni-Awakening-veterans

Phillips, R. Cody, *Operation Joint Guardian: The U.S. Army in Kosovo*, Washington, D.C.: U.S. Army Center of Military History, 2007. As of April 28, 2021:
https://history.army.mil/html/books/070/70-109-1/cmhPub_70-109-1.pdf

Pietz, Tobias, "Demobilization and Reintegration of Former Soldiers in Post-war Bosnia and Herzegovina: An Assessment of External Assistance," mimeo, 2004. As of April 28, 2021:
https://d-nb.info/1007327227/34

Pike, John, "Kosovo Liberation Army [KLA]," webpage, GlobalSecurity, undated. As of April 28, 2021:
https://www.globalsecurity.org/military/world/para/kla.htm

Prados, Alfred B., *Iraqi Challenges and U.S. Military Responses: March 1991 Through October 2002*, Washington, D.C.: Congressional Research Service, RL31641, November 20, 2002.

Qehaja, Ramadan, Kosum Kosumi, and Florian Qehaja, "The Process of Demobilization and Integration of Former Kosovo Liberation Army Members—Kosovo's Perspective," Prishtina, Kosovo: Kosovar Center for Security Studies, April 2010.

Razoux, Pierre, *The Iran-Iraq War*, trans. Nicholas Elliott, Cambridge, Mass.: Belknap Press of Harvard University Press, 2015.

Reddy, Peter, "Reconciliation in Bougainville: Civil War, Peacekeeping and Restorative Justice," *Contemporary Justice Review*, Vol. 11, No. 2, June 2008, pp. 117–130. As of April 28, 2021:
https://www.tandfonline.com/doi/pdf/10.1080/10282580802057744?needAccess=true

Rubin, Michael, "How the United States Could Lose Iraq," *National Interest*, September 21, 2019. As of April 28, 2021:
https://nationalinterest.org/feature/how-united-states-could-lose-iraq-82351

Rudolf, Inna, *The Hashd's Popular Gambit: Demystifying PMU Integration in Post-IS Iraq*, London: International Centre for the Study of Radicalisation, King's College London, 2019. As of February 6, 2021:
https://icsr.info/wp-content/uploads/2019/11/ICSR-Report-The-Hashd's-Popular-Gambit-Demystifying-PMU-Integration-in-Post%E2%80%91IS-Iraq.pdf

Schroeder, Ursula C., and Fairlie Chappuis, "New Perspectives on Security Sector Reform: The Role of Local Agency and Domestic Politics," *International Peacekeeping*, Vol. 21, No. 2, 2014, pp. 133–148. As of April 28, 2021:
https://www.tandfonline.com/doi/full/10.1080/13533312.2014.910401

Schulhofer-Wohl, Jonah, and Nicholas Sambanis, *Disarmament, Demobilization, and Reintegration Programs: An Assessment*, Sandöverken, Sweden: Folke Bernadotte Academy, 2010.

Schwarz, Benjamin C., *American Counterinsurgency Doctrine and El Salvador: The Frustrations of Reform and the Illusions of Nation Building*, Santa Monica, Calif.: RAND Corporation, R-4042-USDP, 1991. As of April 28, 2021:
https://www.rand.org/pubs/reports/R4042.html

Segovia, Alexander, *Transitional Justice and DDR: The Case of El Salvador*, New York: International Center for Transitional Justice, June 2009. As of April 28, 2021:
https://www.ictj.org/sites/default/files/ICTJ-DDR-ElSalvador-CaseStudy-2009-English.pdf

Silva, Graciosa, "General Elections: Opposition Committed to a Coalition That Changes the Course of Democracy 45 Years Later," *Ver Angola*, January 14, 2021. As of February 6, 2021:
https://www.verangola.net/va/en/012021/Politics/23555/General-elections-opposition-committed-to-a-coalition-that-changes-the-course-of-democracy-45-years-later.htm

Simpson, Chris, "Obituary: Jonas Savimbi, Unita's Local Boy," BBC News, February 25, 2002. As of April 28, 2021:
http://news.bbc.co.uk/2/hi/africa/264094.stm

Skinner, Helena, "Why Iraqis Are Protesting After 'Years of Anger and Frustration,'" *EuroNews*, April 10, 2019. As of April 28, 2021:
https://www.euronews.com/2019/10/04/why-iraqis-are-protesting-after-years-of-anger-and-frustration

Smith, Crispin, "After Soleimani Killing, Iran and Its Proxies Recalibrate in Iraq," *Just Security*, February 27, 2020. As of February 6, 2021:
https://www.justsecurity.org/68888/after-soleimani-killing-iran-and-its-proxies-recalibrate-in-iraq/

———, "Iraq's Raid on Iran-Backed Militias: Is the New Prime Minister Ready to Rein Them In?" *Just Security*, July 16, 2020. As of February 6, 2021:
https://www.justsecurity.org/71438/iraqs-raid-on-iran-backed-militias-is-the-new-prime-minister-ready-to-rein-them-in/

Smyth, Phillip, *Iranian Militias in Iraq's Parliament: Political Outcomes and U.S. Response*, Washington, D.C.: Washington Institute for Near East Policy, June 11, 2018. As of April 28, 2021:
https://www.washingtoninstitute.org/policy-analysis/view/iranian-militias-in-iraqs-parliament-political-outcomes-and-u.s.-response

South African History Online, "The Angolan Civil War (1975–2002): A Brief History," webpage, undated. As of April 28, 2021:
https://www.sahistory.org.za/article/angolan-civil-war-1975-2002-brief-history

Staniland, Paul, "States, Insurgents, and Wartime Political Orders," *Perspectives on Politics*, Vol. 10, No. 2, June 2012, pp. 243–264.

———, "Armed Politics and the Study of Intrastate Conflict," *Journal of Peace Research*, Vol. 54, No. 4, 2017, pp. 459–467. As of April 28, 2021:
https://journals.sagepub.com/doi/full/10.1177/0022343317698848

Torjesen, Stina, and S. Neil MacFarlane, "R Before D: The Case of Post Conflict Reintegration in Tajikistan," *Conflict, Security and Development*, Vol. 7, No. 2, 2007, pp. 311–332. As of April 28, 2021:
https://www.tandfonline.com/doi/pdf/10.1080/14678800701333192

UNIFEM—*See* United Nations Development Fund for Women.

"Unita Rebels Sold Diamonds Worth 4 Billion Dollars," Pan African News Agency, June 27, 2000. As of April 27, 2021:
https://reliefweb.int/report/angola/unita-rebels-sold-diamonds-worth-4-billion-dollars

United Nations Security Council, Resolution 1244, S/RES/1244 (1999), June 10, 1999. As of April 28, 2021:
https://peacemaker.un.org/sites/peacemaker.un.org/files/990610_SCR1244%281999%29.pdf

United Nations Department of Peacekeeping Operations, *Second Generation Disarmament, Demobilization, and Reintegration (DDR) Practices in Peace Operations: A Contribution to the New Horizon Discussion on Challenges and Opportunities for UN Peacekeeping*, New York: United Nations, 2010. As of April 28, 2021:
https://peacekeeping.un.org/sites/default/files/2gddr_eng_with_cover.pdf

United Nations Development Fund for Women, *Getting It Right, Doing It Right: Gender and Disarmament, Demobilization and Reintegration*, New York: United Nations, 2004. As of April 28, 2021:
http://www.poa-iss.org/CASAUpload/Members/Documents/
15@Getting_it_Right_Doing_it_Right.pdf

U.S. Central Intelligence Agency, "The Military Balance in Namibia: An Intelligence Assessment," April 1982.

Vines, Alex, and Bereni Oruitemeka, "Bullets to Ballots: The Reintegration of UNITA in Angola: Analysis," *Conflict, Security and Development*, Vol. 8, No. 2, 2008, pp. 241–263. As of April 28, 2021:
https://www.tandfonline.com/doi/full/10.1080/14678800802095385

von Dyck, Christopher, *DDR and SSR in War-to-Peace Transition*, London: Ubiquit Press, 2016.

"Who Are the Northern Alliance?" BBC News, November 13, 2001. As of April 27, 2021:
http://news.bbc.co.uk/2/hi/south_asia/1652187.stm